Praise for *Neither Mountain Nor River*

An engaging, inspiring, heart-filled account of a man's long journey from a childhood filled with trees and fish and birds and bugs to a stay-at-home dad living in the urban east, determined that his children, too, might learn how water flows and muskrats swim, and should thrill at the sight of a trout taking a fly or a rare black-and-white warbler hunting insects at a playground in Queens.

—James R. Babb, Editor, *Gray's Sporting Journal*

In *Neither Mountain nor River*, Mike Freeman, who calls himself a "tireless God-chaser," helps us to see, in his richly numinous descriptions, how both the "insignificant springs, streams, ponds and lakeshores" of Pennsylvania and the sublime wilderness of Alaska's Yakutat River are both part of a creation that has complexity and purpose and, more importantly, all we need, to find the home we long for.

—Robert Cording, Barrett Professor in
Creative Writing at Holy Cross College

In *Neither Mountain Nor River*, Mike Freeman artfully unfolds the way that human love and memory produce a flow of connection from one generation to another, how we can be taught to open our eyes to what is rich and alive in the natural world, as we learn how to be with each other and with nature. This lyrical exploration of faith and learning to see is steeped in the wisdom he received from his beloved father, and which he in turn gifts to his young daughters, as well as the lucky reader.

—Maria Mutch, author of *Know the Night:
A Memoir of Survival in the Small Hours*

D1495307

Mike Freeman's book is a paean to the healing, bonding powers of nature. I frequently found myself lost in his words, which often approached poetry.

— John Lionberger, author of *Renewal in the Wilderness: A Spiritual Guide to Connecting with God in the Natural World.*

Rich and intricately woven as the land, this book unfolds like a prayer: a meditation on life and death and the mysterious nature of the fertile, lovely, terrible world of which we are part.

—Tovar Cerulli, author of *The Mindful Carnivore: A Vegetarian's Hunt for Sustenance*

NEITHER MOUNTAIN NOR RIVER

ALSO BY MIKE FREEMAN

Drifting: Two Weeks on the Hudson

NEITHER MOUNTAIN NOR RIVER

Fathers, Sons, and an Unsettled Faith

Mike Freeman

Publisher's Cataloging-in-Publication

Freeman, Mike, 1968-
    Neither mountain nor river : fathers, sons, and an
unsettled faith / Mike Freeman.
    pages cm
    LCCN 2014936979
    ISBN 978-0-9847927-8-8 (trade paper)
    ISBN 978-0-9847927-9-5 (eBook)

    1. Freeman, Mike, 1968– 2. Fathers and sons—United
States—Biography. 3. Nature. 4. Human ecology—United
States. 5. Outdoor life—United States.   I. Title.

CT275.F74A3 2014   306.874'2'0922

QBI14-600070

Portions of this book have previously appeared in alternate form in *South Dakota Review, Gettysburg Review, The Massachusetts Review, Connecticut Review,* Gray's *Sporting Journal, North Dakota Quarterly, South Loop Review,* and *Weber: The Contemporary West.*

Some of the names in this memoir have been changed.

Introduction clip-art courtesy of Florida Center for Instructional Technology

Riddle Brook Publishing LLC, Bedford NH
www.riddlebrookpublishing.com
www.mikewfreeman.com

For Flannery, Karen, and Shannon

Contents

INTRODUCTION

And Ruth said, Intreat me not to leave thee, or to return from following after thee: for whither thou goest, I will go; and where thou lodgest, I will lodge: thy people shall be my people, and thy God my God.

—RUTH 1:16

I HADN'T LEARNED MUCH in five months of parenting, or even the thirteen of acclimating to city life, but I had learned school schedules. September had finally arrived, with the return to classes reinstating what passed for tranquility in the otherwise bustling Queens neighborhood.

The playground's square half-block provided comparative quiet for the first time since June, with most children now padding about the asphalt on uncertain legs, circling back to a parent's oaken thighs and gentle praise. Others, like mine, were clumps of passive-eyed immobility dandled on a knee or limp in a stroller. With no school, July and August had no respite. All day the rage and glee of more agile kids ran rough-shod over jungle gyms and contested swing space, with the eldest posed along cyclone fences walling out a sheet metal shop and three veins of traffic, fumbling through their budding rebellion and clunky sexuality. While still wrapped in summer heat, though, these first school days again provided a lull, and parents of infants and toddlers filtered in like water before dismissal bells chased us out.

Life comes at you fast, my father says, but until a woman I hardly knew called from four-thousand miles away to announce her pregnancy, I'd managed forty years scarcely scraped by such experience. No matter how lucky the life, however, or nimble the navigation, circumstance eventually checkmates, and life indeed comes at you fast.

Having lived the last ten years in a fly-in only Alaskan village, as close to childhood fantasy as any might achieve, I tumbled back east, to Queens, New York, where in short order I'd become a stay-at-home parent. Mostly this was happy news, as a child was something I and my pending wife Karen had independently coveted. Yet neither of us anticipated the sudden pregnancy nor each other's inevitable quirks, and for my part, in combination with leaving an isolated town of seven hundred to an electrified array of ten million, the shocks hadn't gone unnoticed.

Though I grew up fifty-five miles away in a Connecticut suburb, not leaving until I was twenty-seven and that only to Vermont for a couple of years, New York City was every bit the abstraction it would have been had I reared in Tulsa. Combined with a pregnancy-induced co-habitation after a life of three-month relationships, along with the trading of financial independence for full-time parenting, I more than once while walking Queens or riding a subway felt that I had passed through a Martian landscape, barren and strange.

Masculinity-wise, the timing was apt. Karen called in July, 2008, and when I flew back in early August, few prominent minds doubted that collective financial mayhem was imminent. By September none did, and when our daughter Shannon was born in March, much of the country, particularly New York, was workless. From high finance to construction men took the brunt, and one-to-one ratios were common playground arithmetic as I groped toward familiarity with the now-slumping, now-flailing, always peculiar creature strapped to my chest.

With or without this tacit companionship, though, assumptive role propriety likely wouldn't have chafed me. Money needs to be made, kids need to be raised, with equal weight accorded each. If once I supported myself, I was now tending a child, and any nagging atavism provoked by a diaper change was a meager adjustment. Others, however, were formidable, and tramping the several neighborhoods between the East River and Karen's block all spring and summer, wending diluted ethnic redoubts amidst the barbed-wired, broken-windowed industrial senescence just in from the river, I realized what all new parents do—that many pre-child pursuits, if not lost, were certainly suspended, and might be unrecognizable once that moratorium dissolved.

Retrospectively, then, and prior to becoming a parent myself, my father and I over several decades maintained certain rituals and initiated others, all of them woods-bound. Hunting, fishing, and trapping provided the mediums, but their considerable valence consisted of the same narcotic effervescence of blood, spirit, and the natural world that binds so many families up in wilderness traditions. Such ether coagulates in decidedly palpable ways and, like numberless others, how I structured everything from familial relationships to morality to cosmology came from first delving northeastern uplands, swamps, and creeks, and, later, Alaskan rainforests and Arizonan deserts. If my father wasn't always there, his influence was, and such experiences were the prime movers in how I defined the world.

By September, with my own child at last more a second language than an alien tongue, her existence, I finally realized, might well have ended this history, or at least shoved it beneath ground for an indeterminate tenure. Accrued by filament throughout summer, this fact finally inculcated on a park bench, where I cradled my waking baby among other floundering fathers. Fortunately, something else occurred, simultaneously triggered, as so many things are, by an otherwise meaningless motion within an otherwise common setting.

The heat hadn't relented, with the spotty foliage of little help. Jaundiced weeks prior to any hint of autumn, the already thinning canopy was little match for sunlight. Though Shan had been holding her head up for two months now, I kept my ten fingers poised along her nape, a lingering habit from her first head-flopping weeks. Still with time before school let out, I nuzzled her up and down on a knee, happy we could roam the small grounds a bit before heading off. More active by the hour, she'd taken to external movement recently, and the city's regnant pigeons and house sparrows were now of great interest. As consciousness re-flooded her, I rose, strapping her face-out in the chest carrier, pointing here to a kid, there to a sparrow as we doddered about.

Centered by a pair of elaborate jungle gyms, the playground's west fence backstopped the swings, while the other barriers were fronted by the many failing pin oaks. Though a popular urban shade choice, it seems they'd pushed the asphalt too close to these upon planting, which now buckled badly around expanded boles, though not enough to properly irrigate the roots below. Sparrows, mostly, used them, flocking in for a few moments, thronging limbs, chatting, defecating, gushing off, while an occasional mockingbird jaunted over from Sunnyside Gardens a few blocks away, bleeding its mimicry over the interred loam before flapping forth. The pigeons scarcely perched here, dominating the ground, pilfering abandoned crusts and tattered fruit bars.

Though still adjusting to what few birds Queens offered compared with those that Alaska did, I'd come to know that jewels could be found, and ambled Shan around to have a look.

With the help of her bottom-balancing father, I watched a severally-braided girl climb a slide, unsure of foot or hand purchases. Though riveted for a time, Shan abruptly pulled her eyes off the girl toward the nearest oak. Though no tree had produced acorns, squirrels still visited, popping through tears in the back fence where a hodgepodge strip of sycamore, oak, maple, and cherry saplings screened the sheet metal shop. This one was half-way up a trunk, stopping, starting, turreting its head, scuttling a bit further. It gained a limb, righted itself, scratched the bark, then put front paws to yearning lips, lapping an acorn that wasn't there. Shannon's eyes followed, her face broadening to a two-toothed smile, while three trees away my own attention was drawn to a different movement. Slashed with rills of black and white, a bird jittered along a limb, bounced a little further, then flittered to the trunk, several times clefting the bark before rounding the tree and appearing again. City-bound or not, these moribund oaks havened insects, colonies of them, something southbound September bird migrants would surely know.

"Good God," I said. "Black-and-white warbler."

Though I'd only seen maybe a dozen in my life, all but the first did the same thing, bustled me back to the shaded deck of a lakefront cabin, where my father introduced me to bird life.

No one has fingered why birds arouse such pleasure, such pinpoint intimacy within our generic attractions to nature, but they do. It's possible I would have been pulled to them without my father, but he bound me to birds early on and in critical ways they've remained a similar tie binding the two of us.

Pennsylvania started it. When my older sisters were toddlers, my parents bought a cabin there on a small lake, tucked in the Endless Mountains, a largely unknown segment between the more famous Poconos to the south and New York's Catskills to the north. A decade later, when my pop came up from our Connecticut home on summer weekends, I'd sit with

8

him, quietly, while he drank morning tea on the hardwood-shrouded deck, the lake out front obscured by leaves and trunks, viburnum and blackberry veiling the shore. Up in the sun-shot maple and ash canopy we rarely saw more than a fussy silhouette, but my dad knew their songs and it was those names, the words, that first sucked me in, passing through his lips while the eyes stayed up, roving.

More often than not he just had the warbled notes, and every few minutes he'd issue his own strange syllables: Red-eyed vireo. Blue-gray gnat-catcher. Cedar waxwing. Great-crested fly-catcher. Black-billed cuckoo. Eastern towhee. Wood pewee. Ovenbird. Black-throated green warbler. Hermit thrush. Swainson's thrush. Phoebe. Rose-breasted grosbeak. Golden-crowned kinglet. Orchard oriole.

Birds, then, helped cinch us, and in the decades to come that knot only strengthened. Whether hunting or fishing, walking or playing catch, there was always bird life about, so much so that by the time he visited Alaska each October to hunt ducks, the fall migrants we saw while paddling a canoe or wading swamps were like thumbing three decades' worth of diaries, with each species towing with it a referential collage.

Animals, of course, paralleled this, particularly when he revived his childhood love of muskrat trapping once I turned twelve, buying a dozen footholds and taking me out to a few strings of Connecticut golf course ponds to set them all fall and winter. We didn't catch anything, but our failure only honed that desideratum, not only prompting us to expand our Connecticut territory, but to trap around the Pennsylvania cabin as well. Escalating our efforts over thirty years—right through Shannon's birth—we spent the week surrounding Thanksgiving there running a mink and muskrat trap line all morning while hunting grouse and woodcock each afternoon, and such habits transferred. After a couple of years in Vermont, I moved West in rough accord with my dad's own relocation, and for ten years we traded weeks visiting each other in Alaska and Arizona, hunting ducks in the former while ambling deserts in the latter, simply watching. Through all the seismic, wildly various 'You're-going-to-be-a-father' percussion, it took a year to recognize that these traditions were gone, likely for good, and yet a few ounces of feather and sinew in an asphalt-encased park reminded me that such losses would not elicit the shock I once anticipated. "Look, Shannon. Look," I said, pointing, stepping closer.

If that bird skitched a pin oak in Queens, for at least a flash it scratched along the lake cabin's roof corner, where my pop had heard it, twisting in his chair for a peak. "Jesus, Mike," he'd said. "Look."

I did look, at the same black and white rills streaking the strange, stout little bird first needling gutter compost, then hanging upside down along the roof joint, hoping to nip a moth or spider lodged behind the flood light. It succeeded, flying off with some undisclosed insect. We traced the ascent before it lost itself in a tupelo crown shading the next cabin over. My dad spoke.

"That was a black and white warbler. It's too early for migration. That guy must have nested here. They're deep woods birds, so you rarely get that close a look. Great stuff."

I might have been eight. In the years and decades to come came the constant reminders from friends, family, and external professionals to weigh against disaster, to bank enough reserves so as to weather any significant financial trauma. We do the best we can, and though I'd walked out of Alaska with enough money to contribute to a family budget a while, such matters were often a befuddlement. From childhood on, however, I'd always had great fidelity to the concept when applied to memory. Experience informs it all, cementing relationships while tendering material for our bricolage worldviews. Through my father, then, whether with him or alone, I'd deposited more than enough poignant, pleasant recollection to withstand that significant loss, and while domesticity certainly isn't a catastrophe, by its nature it does sever vital cables.

Nudging Shan, I reared back a bit, properly angling her head, watching the bird lurch off the oak in search of insects before the southbound file along an uncertain coast.

"Look, honey. Black and white warbler. Right there."

God knows what she saw, but it didn't matter. I could accrue a new principle now with my own child, equally pleased that whatever loss I felt at relinquishing traditions I thought would last through my pop's death would be profoundly mollified, softened by payouts from all those memories we'd acquired. Barbara Fields, a historian, paraphrased William

Faulkner when she said that "history isn't *was*, it's *is*." If unsure of the push-off into marriage and fathering, then, I knew I could always rely on the comforting keel that my own *is* would provide, a ballast in which I'd perpetually wallow.

A PRIORI

I know that He exists.
Somewhere—in silence—
He has hid his rare life
From our gross eyes.

—EMILY DICKINSON

If I saw a Louisiana water thrush today I probably couldn't name it. From where it was, by how it behaved, I might piece together what I know from memory and make the proper guess, but I haven't seen one in forty years.

I've only witnessed one my whole life, long ago as a boy, when my father walked me down the Coxton Lake outlet in northeastern Pennsylvania, a waterbody straddling the divide of the Susquehanna and Delaware Rivers. They're a tiny creature, half-shorebird, half-songbird, diddling about the edges of waterways, hunting up nymph life. With a brown back and buff underbelly they're somewhat sparrow-like, but beyond that my knowledge of them is nil. Myth, though, doesn't require much detail, flourishing just fine without it. It's not the thrush, then, that has supplied such sparing clarity, but the image of my father, in his prime, pointing it out. It's this that's become mythical, and my own private bastion—however false—when the prospect of age and death for the people I know comes too close.

Like a great many sons I couldn't spend enough time with my dad when I was young. That changes with adolescence, of course, but until that transition most boys crave the company of their father. In my case, during summer breaks, that company was sparse but intense. My sisters, mother, and I spent July and August at the lake, a time going by like most summer days, slow and easy. During the week I'd swim, fish, and tramp the woods with friends, but mostly I'd anticipate Friday night, when long after I should've been asleep I'd hear my father's car come down the driveway. I didn't get him the whole weekend, but I got him enough, and it was when we took to the woods that the world grew both bigger and smaller all at once.

Birth order may or may not matter, but I never blamed it for anything. The only boy of my parents' three kids, I was additionally the youngest, born far enough behind my two sisters that I had the benefits of a sibling while experiencing at least in part what an only child must.

Born in the late '30s around Philadelphia, my parents met at a school mixer, stayed together through college, then married when my pop graduated in 1960. As was common back then, one daughter came the next year, when my mom was twenty-one, and the other two years later. Each delivery was complicated, and doctors counseled that she cease at two. She wanted a boy, though, and five years and a couple of miscarriages later she had one. Three years beyond that, in 1971, my father quit his sales job with a major firm to try his own hand at business, starting a consulting outfit with three other guys, and my parents moved us to Wilton, Connecticut, where we remained. Like so many people, my mother struggled with full-time parenting, foregoing a promising start in juvenile court reform in Philadelphia to make the move to New England. Summers we spent at the lake in Pennsylvania, in the cabin they'd bought not long after their second daughter was born. Rural, quiet, and forested, the place was an idyll, and with my sisters entering teenage independence while I was still a child, I often had one parent or another to myself.

Nature was everything to me then, and without organized activities of any kind, summer in Pennsylvania was the time to plunge. Every rock turned over in the lake uncovered crayfish and bullheads, leeches and dragonfly nymphs, while pollywogs and minnows hid amongst the lily pads, hiding from the bass and pickerel that lurked in the depths. The woods, too, were filled, sheltering birds and animals of every kind, and my father seemed to know all there was to know. Sometimes we'd see something, maybe a deer or blue jay, but mostly he pointed out sign, fox scat, say, or last year's warbler nest. Each day out brought new knowledge, and with every bit dispensed, my penchant to be around him grew in kind. He was strong then, tireless, and could walk all day, and if I'd had my childish wish we would've taken a few scant items with us one morning and simply lived out there, learning, a restive wonderment that for better or worse I retained in perpetuity. In the meantime, I was certainly still a child, when any memory, no matter how seemingly insignificant at the time, can imprint deep enough to resonate for life.

Weekends on the lake were crowded and the midday heat drew boat traffic. The preferred hours were later, before the long summer sun had weakened but after most boaters grew weary. A calm fell on the day then, when old men rowed out to their bass holes and other people sunned themselves on the docks. The outlet side of the lake was undeveloped, and that's where my dad took me to quietly probe the shoreline.

The creek itself is a hop-across affair running dry most of the summer. Through the deeper forest, beavers had built a pond where we went hiking too, but we spent most of our time around the stream mouth—just inside the trees, out in a boat fishing, or wading the lakeshore. Crayfish sheltered under the rocks, and while I turned over what I could, I relished when my father was there, heaving up the heaviest of them where most of the crabs lay. They'd scuttle backward or stand in defense with their pincers held high. He had more patience than me and caught them in droves, holding them with two fingers so I could inspect. Bullhead mothers, as well, stood guard over their broods, compact balls of little black bodies swirling among the lily pads, and often a kingfisher perched itself in an overhang, lording over the shallows. Nearly every day, too, raccoon tracks sullied the ancient glacial sands. My dad would point them out, explaining why they were there, and each time a little more of the world was revealed. Nearly all of these images run together now, muddled in the oneiric solution of childhood memory. A few, though, have congealed.

On one point my pop was predictable. His movements changed whenever he saw something rare. Whether we were in the woods or the water the language was always the same. He paused, held still, then edged his head forward, allowing his weak eyes greater focus. One day, with the sun out and a faint breeze tickling the water mid-lake we approached the outlet, feebly trickling away before vanishing in mud and dry rock. My dad was about ten yards from me, wading deeper in the lily pads looking for pollywogs while I poked near the shore for crayfish. I had my head down, looking for a loose rock to turn over when he stopped. I squared myself to him, then turned my head to see what he saw. Alder and birch saplings crowded the shore near the outlet here, reaching out over the lake's open space for sunlight. Tucked beneath these tiny trunks was the shore itself, a narrow strip of dark sand and rock. Green reeds poked up between the stones, and amidst all this there was movement, a little brown bird scuttling in short bursts, stopping every four skips or so to pry its needly bill in sand. Several times it hopped up into the braid of old leaves left by high-water events, nudging these as well. I looked back at my dad. He was still studying, squinting to ward off the glare. His eyes—clear and searching—never left the bird. Raising a thickly-veined arm, he pointed right at it.

"Look," he said. "There. A Louisiana water thrush."

I was young then, a child, assuming my father knew everything, and this cinched it. How could anyone point to a bird that looked like a hundred others and say without hesitation "Louisiana water thrush"?

"'You see it?" he said. "There? They're a little like sandpipers, only smaller and more shy."

Now I had *sandpipers*, too, another term I didn't know. We watched until it reached the outlet mouth, where it turned for a look then flew off down the dry channel.

I've never seen one since.

My dad followed it as far as he could, but I mostly just watched him watching the bird. The sun was still bright and cut neatly around him on either side, producing something indelible, even artistic. My father was in his prime, mid-thirties, when the mind has finally learned what the body can do and works with it in great efficiency for a short, grand span before the joints and muscles begin their long, collective decline. The broad shoulders, which still carried me through tangled stretches of forest, narrowed down his tanned torso to his hips. His arms hung low in a jungly manner and were capable, I knew, of great things. It was the mind, though, that held it all. Inside that head, following the flight path of the thrush, was a vast reservoir, a place I could always go to gather knowledge. It never occurred to me then that my father would grow old. It didn't occur to me that anyone I knew would grow old. I know better now, but as years passed and I witnessed the slow decay of not only my father's body but my own and those of friends and family, I had that image to fall back on. Death and the fearsome mysteries that attend it are inevitable, but when the rot in ourselves and the people close to us becomes too evident we can override it with a thought, finding enough peace beneath this aegis to hammer out a happy life.

My dad and I never met Smiley Slater, never saw him nor heard his voice, and felt fortunate that the myth never became man.

"You can trap there if you want," Mr. Wainright had said, "but don't let Smiley catch you. He's three-hundred pounds, most of which can and wants to do you harm, even to people who live around here if they're on his land."

Mr. Wainright's father had built the lake cabin my parents eventually bought, and by rural rite his son Carl became the one to call for upkeep. My pop wouldn't have had it any other way. Country-decent and country-wise, Carl is the gentlest man I've known, despite the rough leather sixty years of carpentry had rendered his palms and fingers.

He also possessed the only mind I'd ever crossed that made no distinction between the world's beauty and utility. For Carl, the world is beautiful because it's useful, useful because it's beautiful, with no partition separating the two.

"Look at that," he once said, running two fingers along a tongue-and-groove board cut to size.

My mom was inside the cabin, having called Carl days before to mend a burst pipe on the lone outbuilding, a bunkhouse he'd built to summer my now-adolescent sisters. The repair required cutting away three boards outside the bathroom, beneath which yellow jackets had nested, colonizing a ground hole. Carl sprayed them down, allowing him to work, and had me watch the now poisoned nest as he lay on his back half beneath the elevated dwelling, flanging and soldering pipe. That done, he simply needed to replace the boards and paint.

"You see that grain?" he said, kneeling. "That's sugar maple, the same tree that brings you syrup. Lord, that's pretty."

The plank was three feet long, not much shorter than me, and I ran a pair of fingers half its length as he had done. Thorough planing validated his observation, with sorrel threads wavering lengthwise along the blanched yellow field, accumulating to compact, annulated gyres where burls or branch starts had been sanded smooth. Carl, though, knew more.

"This is just what the mill gives us. You should see them off the stump. These little brown lines? Here? They're rings when the tree's in the round. Brush away the saw chips and you can age any tree by the ring number, but with these it's the pattern that gets you. The wood is nearly white. And maples mostly make autumn so nice. You'll come up here hunting soon with your dad every fall. When you do, look over these mountains in

October. Nearly all that red you'll see is from this wood, right here, orange too."

He turned the board over, pivoting on his knees and balancing it with two hands, pressing it against existing studs while sliding the top ridge into the groove of the red board above. His left fist held it in place while the right slipped a dozen nearly headless nails out of a hip pouch, most going into his mouth. Up came the hammer, a tap and two whacks per nail times six, all repeated with the two boards remaining. Finished, he squatted back.

"There. A little primer, a little paint, and she's all set."

Carl introduced us to Smiley, or at least his land, but only from the road, and that only in passing by. Having trout fished up here for twenty years along with hunting ducks, grouse, and woodcock, my dad knew the country well, and though he'd stopped trapping as a teenager, his love for it never died, only cocooned. When our second season approached when I was thirteen, then, he knew of at least a few places surrounding the lake house where we could set traps—generally just called *sets*—for muskrats over holiday breaks, an occasion that quickly evolved into Thanksgiving and New Year's traditions.

He mentioned this looming interest to Carl, who delighted. Reared here, Carl had grown up trapping the creeks and ponds all around, only stopping when his own children siphoned off what little free time remained. "Trapping was always my favorite," I remember him saying. "You're out there every morning, every day, quiet, never knowing what you'll find or what you'll see. Hunting and fishing are ok, but trapping's different. You almost feel like you're part of it."

Sometime in August he drove us around, along the red clay roads and lightly traveled two-lanes transecting the wooded hills and dairy-dying valleys, pointing to springlets, stretches of stream, mountaintop beaver ponds, all bits of land whose place-names would become our step stones, pathways to inner shrines. Charlie's. Lepro's Bridge. Buck's Meadow. Dunn Pond. Camp Wayne. Bannicky's. Glover's. The Upper Equinunk. The Lower Equinunk. Mount Tone. The Gravel Pit. Cory's Creek. Shehawken, Upper and Lower.

Because of Smiley, Smiley's never made the roster, but we did give it a shot. Driving by, Carl hung a hand out of his pickup, pointing down a sharp drop through the bunched aspen where the Starrucca River—just a creek, maybe ten yards wide, never over your head—cut between a cornfield and the steep incline back to the road.

"That's great territory," he said. "Mink, muskrat, coon, beaver. A friend snuck in a few fox sets along that corn, too, I think ten years ago. He got a couple of reds, maybe a gray, but Smiley caught up with him, or at least chased him out of there. Joe was checking his sets, and here comes Smiley, mid-November, stomping across that creek, swearing up a storm. Joe saw him through the hedge and took off running. He'd parked halfway up the mountain along the old railroad bed. Smiley was too big to chase him long, but Joe lost those traps. As far as I know no one's been down there since."

My pop was born in 1937, likely the last generation raised to prescription WASP refinement. Prep schools, Yale, Harvard Business, the works. Fate rarely suits up the right ball player, though, as my dad is far more one part Huck Finn to one part Tom Sawyer than any pre-ordained Skull-and-Bones man. Subsequently, though I was too young to know it in the pickup, at some later point I realized that upon the words "no one's been down there since" we were most assuredly going to trap Smiley Slater's creek that fall.

Though I would acquire parcels of my father's derring-do, I'd never match it, and at thirteen had none. That November, sensing my anxiety on the drive up from Connecticut, he said "Don't worry. We'll walk down from the railroad cut to set, then use the drop-off plan to check. The guy won't know a thing."

He'd devised the drop-off plan in Connecticut. This was the state's southwest corner, toward New York. Though politically conservative it's rabidly anti-trapping, and even where we had permission we checked our traps at night, with my pop dropping me off while he drove in a circle, rightly calculating that one dark figure would be harder to spot than two and a parked car. Knowing we'd use this plan at Smiley's put me somewhat at ease, as did the thought of plump, plush, swamp-rank muskrats. Unlike the previous season, we'd had some success running the golf course sets that October, along with a couple of soft-banked stretches of the Norwalk River, an otherwise rock-strewn Connecticut stream. One morning, fog-bound, two hours prior to work and school, it happened. My dad waded into a watercress-fluffed springlet feeding a cattail marsh, fumbling along a dark bank for a dark trap.

"It's gone," he said, cautiously fingering the muskrat den's lip.

Two days before, on opening day, he'd put his arm inside to the elbow and hauled out a knotted wad of green, incisor-nipped rushes.

"That means it's active. Put your hand up there. Feel the smooth sides?"

Now he hooked the trap wire with a chilled finger and pulled as I stepped off the bank. Up it came, drowned, pinched by a front leg, all in silhouette from what scant light the droplet fog reflected.

"Muskrat," my dad said. "Congratulations."

Depressing the trap spring, he had me remove the creature, stiff and taut. Though I could barely see, the weight was enough, wrapped in wet, warm fur.

Later the color would come, the same from all the photos in all the articles I'd gorged that summer with an amateur's appetite. The ginger-touched browns, founded by gray wool beneath, what muskrats salve with oils to press water out as they swim, would emerge. With none of this visible now, the weight alone did it, the weight and the fur and the perfume of chill and mud and autumn-decayed vegetation, along with the inextricably flummoxed arousal of killing something you revere. I'd be a trapper, then, for life, with even Smiley's three-hundred pounds unable to deflect the promise of new country.

All started well. Nervy, but well. After setting a few of our safer zones, places where my father had good relationships with the farmers, we headed up the mountain well upstream of Smiley's then turned again, mid-slope, following the unkept cinder byway where scarcely a tie remained of the old railroad track and the old railroad days. Three miles down we parked, switch-backing the forested hillside to the broad creek flat below.

"We'll head to where the Starrucca runs tight to the slope, upstream of that cornfield," my pop said. "That way we can use the creek brush to avoid crossing open ground."

The rainless weeks prior helped us out, that and the fact that we could walk the stubbled field while being screened by the hedge. Once level with where we needed to cross, the low water made a simple ford.

With each of us shouldering a brace of traps strung over a trowel handle, we spread out amongst the grid of rivulets and diminutive ponds that beavers had made of the original sprin-glets feeding the Starrucca. My dad knew it then and I would recognize such things soon, but to anyone harboring high affection for muskrats and mink, this place was Shambhala. Pill-sized, clay-like muskrat pellets dotted the dry rocks and half-submerged logs, while cuttings—the clipped grasses 'rats drop on their to and fro endeavors—littered each flowage coming off the beaver dams. Though the image of an apoplectic farmer never left my mind, with Smiley's now herdless dairy farm a mile up the pike and the high bank above veiling any road travelers, I was able to revel in our newfound territory, along with the anticipation each set trap sowed. After an hour two dozen were in. We re-crossed the stream, followed the hedge, then ascended the ridge to the car. At night we'd take a different approach.

At that time, Pennsylvania opened mink and muskrat season on Thanksgiving morning, the day we set, and our subsequent Thursday and Friday night checks passed without incident. My father scarcely stopped where Carl had pointed, and popping out, I more skied than walked the steep, clay-slick slope. Despite a mackerel sky one night and cloud cover the next, I ran every set without a flashlight. Two muskrats on Thursday, three on Friday, easy as pie.

The one variable we never added in Connecticut, however, since we didn't have to, was deer season, a foolish omission in Pennsylvania. On Saturday night, though, we remained innocent, and by the time I slipped out of the car and down the hill, muskrats alone were my focus.

Snug beneath the clouds, a bit of humidity had descended, and I realized I'd layered on one too many shirts. The heavy air held the beavers' castor stench, too, a simultaneously acrid and slightly sweet scent used to mark territory.

Our bottom sets guarded two springlets entering the main stem, and starting there I worked up the dendritic sloughs, weaving in and out of thick sapling growth promoted by persistent beaver mowings. Darker than the previous nights, I needed the flashlight, cupping the lens to emit only what was necessary. Removing a drowned 'rat from a feedbed above the upmost dam, I added it to the first, picked up in a den lower down. With one set left not far off, the woods and the creek and the sheared corn beyond lit up in immediate, fluorescent day.

It happened so fast, we say. *There was only time to react.* Occasionally that's true. A stand of pickup-mounted flood lights seared the darkness, and whatever confidence I'd built up vanished. Certain an impossibly large and enraged man had my forehead in a rifle scope, I legged the five longest strides of my life toward the light's source and the shield the high incline beneath might provide. Jumping, I landed flush in a multi-floral rose tangle, hung up like a doughboy outside an Argonne trench. The thick, hooked thorns punctured where they could and tore clothes where they couldn't, but no matter. I'd held onto the 'rats, and immobile or not I was just outside the beam's spectacular radius. Still, enough light leaked downhill, and any movement might initiate the cannonade. If I batted an eyelash I don't remember it.

An occasional voice bled out of the diesel throb atop the ridge, but beyond discerning one man's pitch from the other I couldn't apprehend a word. Though my head was down to avoid eye reflection, the shifting shadows said that whoever stood up there was scanning, running that light from one end of the valley to the next, then again. It's only a matter of time, I thought.

As quickly as it had arrived, though, the illumination was gone. Doors slammed, gears shifted, and the scantly-muffled engine faded downvalley. Minutes passed. Eventually, with effort, I extracted myself from the thorns, then checked the last set and made my way uphill. Crouched beneath the sightline, I awaited the gentler lights of my father's car, which soon arrived. Hustling out, I opened the door and climbed in.

"Wow," he said, driving. "Two more? This place is loaded. Your face is bleeding. Must have hit a briar."

"Was that him?" I said. "Was that Smiley? How did he not see me?"

"What? That light? Christ, no. That was just a couple of locals jacking deer, looking for racks before the big day. No sweat."

Sweat it was, though, and while I didn't say a thing, my dad didn't either. I wasn't ready for this and he knew it. The next day, first light, we stealthed downhill from the rail bed to pull our sets, and that was it, the short-happy life of our Smiley's trap line, though it wasn't the last time I'd trespass there.

LATER IN LIFE a few months doesn't mean much, doesn't invoke change great or small, but to a teen such spans ignite one transformation after another. By the following August, then, I'd limbered a bit, able to withstand the prospect of scampering away from Smiley Slater or anyone else, maybe even face them, and in close companionship with this blossoming moxie came the goading incipience of independence, the notion that a life adrift might well beat a life on the docks, or home, with unmooring little more a task than un-cleating a bowline. It's the rite of us all, and begins by simply cracking a door, stepping forth to gauge the winds outside.

I was fourteen now, the standard fulcrum year. The previous fall our first Connecticut muskrats coincided with middle school football. My dad coached, and after a practice he had me sit in the car while he talked to a kid on the high school varsity. Dusk became dark, and sometime later my dad opened the door.

"Sorry about that," he said, pulling onto the road. "I had to talk to John a while."

"Is he ok?"

"He will be. He and his dad are having a tough time. His dad asked me to talk to him."

"What's wrong?"

"Nothing, really. Every kid since Adam eventually hates his father, at least for a couple of years. It'll happen to you too." He threw the car into fourth and eased into the short cruise back home, allowing me digestion.

At thirteen, to me my pop was Apollo, but that conversation was the first time I thought he was wrong. Regardless, by the next summer nothing had happened, and I was pleasantly poised atop the filial piety of before and the more restive will of his prediction to come.

It was also the last summer I'd spend any substantial time in Pennsylvania. In a year I'd have other interests, but with my sisters nineteen and twenty-one and my mother trading time between them at home and me at the lake, I often had days at a stretch to myself.

Whatever I did or didn't learn, I learned that I love to walk and, like my father, could do so nearly without end. Five mile jaunts became eight, eight became twelve, and soon enough fifteen-mile roundtrips were garden variety, all of them barefoot. On roads and off, in deep woods and meadows, by streamsides, lakesides, mountaintops, and valleys, I spent daylight searching for muskrats or fishing for trout, but mostly just walking.

Two days before heading back to Connecticut and school, I left at dawn with no place in mind, and certainly not Smiley's. By early afternoon, though, having bent south at Starrucca Village a couple of hours before, I passed the big man's farm, which was rapidly converting to what so many others had already—a hive for bats, bees, spiders, and voles, but little else. A parked pickup blocked the house driveway, but other than a listing vane nothing moved. A mile down brought the same drop I'd shakingly hastened months before, and with foliage aplenty and no car or bike to tip me off, I re-descended to the water below.

Though nothing I encountered was awry or unexpected, somewhere in the next hour I portaled into my life's chief pursuit, and while I never found my way back, it would be nearly a lifetime before I realized that I'd crossed any threshold at all.

I know people, several—two doctors, a few teachers, a sculptor, and a pro surfer—who can bull's-eye the youthful moment when they knew passion would wed vocation. I can, too, but it took two decades to acquire that marksmanship, to epiphanize an epiphany I didn't initially see. When recognition finally came, humility attended it, maybe a bit of shame, for when we stop being children we're to put away childish things, something likely for the ill I never did.

Well into my thirties, then, what was soon to abscise

along Smiley's unknown stretch of water would finally germinate, that I'd never pursue a profession, not with any gusto, but would always be and had always been a dogged, tireless God-chaser, with every thrush's song, every woodpecker rattle, every stream riffle and snapped stick in the woods a whirlwind vibration, every foot of earth a potential Peniel, the knoll where Jacob wrestled his angel.

Beavers still plugged the sloughs, their dams further buttressed now with green-leaved limbs, and though fainter than last November, trace castor braided the cow flop scent threaded in from distant pastures. Typical of streamside colonies, none of the several ponds were large, the biggest—in which they'd chosen to lodge—maybe fifteen yards long by five wide. Slogging barefoot, I made for this peeled-log dome risen feet above the surface. Bunched in front, a tangle of green branch shears marked the winter food cache, and upright atop the dwelling I could see beaver droppings lumping its channeled ingress. Indeterminate banks were studded with pencil-point birch, aspen, and cottonwood nubs, all shaded by dense sapling stands that the seed tree razings allowed. The lodge held what I'd hoped to find. Mink scat. Mink work the same territory as muskrats, but as predators their numbers are far less and their roving presence more diffuse. As such, they're difficult to catch, particularly for novices, and their station within our trap line cosmology had already vaulted to mystic. Unlike 'rats, mink leave scant sign, but root around preferred ground long enough and you'll likely turn up a dropping or two. Here one came quickly. Five minutes in and the plaited, pinkie-length fur braid lay atop the first place I checked. Picking it up, I combed out nits of scale and bone that flecked the twisted vole and cottontail fur, noting that the fecal residue had yet to leach off. Trapping season or no, mink infused me, and not twenty-four hours had lapsed since this one had passed through.

Straddling the lodge's apex, I turned to face the brush, pricked by a bird's proximate chips, so distinct from the more innocuous chirps. To date I couldn't identify many species, but this one was simple, feet away and purely primrose.

"Yellow warbler," my father had said a few springs before. "Probably the easiest to ID."

While it was too late for this one to guard a nest, it thoroughly scolded, popping from sapling to sapling, slinging clipped-note scorn my way. Fledglings, likely, flight-wobbled, huddled below, and along with her clarion color she hoped the racket would draw me off. Fair enough. I picked my way down the lodge, breast-stroked the pondlet, then parted the bank brush shielding the Starrucca.

Though I was fully exposed now, neither Smiley nor anyone else ever crossed my mind. Only the long, soothing pool ahead, where the creek composed itself before rounding a corner and rushing the incline along the road, drew my attention. Ragweed and goldenrod had purchased among the rounded stones left bare by summer drought and, as I walked, grasshoppers flung from stalk to stalk, with the goldenrod bobbing up and down with each release. On this bank and that, moreover, upstream and down, the insects that didn't scare quivered out their late-season choral hum, sovereign to the creek water's meeker ripplings. I reached the pool, then crouched.

The brown trout I expected, not the brooks. For decades the Starrucca had been a put-and-take creek, one of thousands nationwide that states stock every April with hatchery fish. Brookies are the East's only native trout, but alongside them the hatcheries dump European browns and American Cascades rainbows. Less aggressive and more sensitive to habitat changes such as forest clearings, brookies haven't done well with competition, and most confine themselves now to mountainside tributaries where transplants don't go. Here, though, lilting in the inert current, I counted five, spaced feet apart in shore-to-shore alignment. The biggest might have been six inches, far too small to have seen a hatchery, and even at this distance I could count the vermicelli squiggles on their green-glow backs.

Five yards ahead rested two browns, side by side and considerably longer. The large, burnt-orange globes amidst the drabber blacks speckling gold sides indicated they were born here, as for reasons unknown hatchery fish have far smaller spots.

The trout remained motionless. Then I stood. With scarcely a body shimmer apiece all seven were gone, shot upstream, with just an ephemeral silt cloud marking the rock crag where each had chosen to hide. Stirred by both the trouts' motion and mine, a denser fish school unraveled in the pool's depths before re-huddling. Sluggish and thick-scaled, these were chubs and shiners, the former gold, the latter silver. More comfortable in ponds and lakes, these had congregated in the most dormant stretch they could find, and by sheer number had pressed the trout back to shallower water. Come night, though, their torpor and that same number would undo them, making far more attractive targets to otters and mink. Still dripping, I stepped creekside and waded in, careful not to quash the myriad caddis larvae spread out over the stones.

The creatures trout eat are as intriguing as the fish themselves. Flip a rock over and any manner of life might be found, wriggling along the underside or dazed in gravel. Maggot-like in color and form, caddis nymphs reside above these rocks, cementing themselves inside twig and sand abodes to shunt predators. Here, nearly every stone hosted three or four. With my soles sliding along the algae-slick rocks, I stopped knee-deep, then bent. Crayfish burrow beneath certain shelters, piling pale, clean sand where they do. Two such telltales girded this particular rock and, fingering an edge, I lifted slowly, trying not to silt-billow anything beneath. Every hoist was like Christmas morning, and this one didn't disappoint.

Not far from the crayfish, a hellgrammite—creek-bottom brown, something like an underwater centipede—arched back its mid-section, protruding pincers from the hard-shell face, arraying for assault. The crayfish—thick, gray, heavily-carapaced—tightened inward to resemble a stone. He'd be easy, I knew, and went right for the fighter.

No less spunky in my palm, the hellgrammite wormed and writhed, pincers poised, seeking something to inflict. These are Dobson fly nymphs, a short-lived, clumsy-flighted insect that emerges for a week to breed after three years underwater.

As hellgrammites, trout adore them, and during high-water events when sudden current strength dislodges a great many, fish often plug their guts where the iron-tough creatures live for some time. I'd slit open several trout stomachs on such days and found a few—mandibles slashing—before releasing them in good health. This one I put back as well, and in the clear, light current watched it drift down, the feathery branchials adorning its sides re-raking oxygen.

Save whisking antennae, the crayfish hadn't moved. I'd caught hundreds in the lake and elsewhere, and left this one alone, letting it imagine that its ruse had worked.

Until now I hadn't realized how hot it was, and despite already being wet and the presence of an escalating breeze, I waded toward the shiner/chub pack and dove, scattering fish. As I re-surfaced I looked downstream, where a couple of dozen harrowed the pool's bottom riffle to escape. Inhaling, I submerged, frog-kicking upstream to the pool head, floating back through with just my sun-bathed face above. Suspended in the calmest stretch, I remained as such for minutes before standing, pivoting as quickly toward the wing burst upstream.

The Starrucca here s-curves, with the pool perpendicular to two swift-water runs. Anything floating down, then, is brush-blind, which was true of the hen wood duck and her four maturing ducklings, all of whom had gained flat water before I rose. Though mature males would have gaudily molted by now, these were mostly black, save the dull-brown, dull-eyed hen, who likely had the beaver ponds in mind, where she and her charges could gambol and feed. Water fell from wings, and as they broke over Smiley's corn before tacking back upstream, the sun caught each blue-iridescent speculum, flickering a bit with each wing flap.

With twelve or more miles of my own to retrace, I noted the dropping sun and clambered back through the ponds and up to the road. Passing Smiley's, I stopped, bothered by what I thought was a bug bite but which turned out to be a leech—gossamer belly bulged with blood—on my calf. Flicking it to the grass, I continued, where well after twilight and a mile from home the anti-coagulants finally abated, allowing the blood flow to stop. Throughout the walk I'd felt inhabited, but I'd be twenty-some years older and four-thousand miles away before I understood by what. In the interim, most everything that would transpire would be subconsciously distilled through that simple creek walk.

INTELLIGENCE IS A WORD, instinct another, and sentient and intuition extend the family. It's intellect, though, that makes the crown, and as human beings we most often feel that it's a crown we alone were given to wear. In the Western tradition, at any rate, that's been true for millennia, and something the Age of Reason not only didn't overthrow but instead strengthened. Though Romantics like Wordsworth and Keats made a gamey revolt of it, Enlightenment thinkers heired us the dominant legacy, where the rest of the animal world is a brutish aggregate. While it's true that notion has suffered recently, the bulk of humanity still sees our kind as the only source of earthly reason and at best assigns to certain animals an elevated instinct. Anyone who spends enough time in the woods, however, can't maintain that position for long. For me, ruffed grouse pulled those walls down years ago.

Ruffed grouse have encompassed my life. Even before

hunting at twelve I'd seen them in the woods, alive, thundering through thickets, or sometimes their stiff, rumpled bodies when my father returned from a hunt. Certain recollections supersede others—two fanned tails in October leaves, or a preening male courting a mate at the edge of an old logging road—but even these are too many to sort. Through a lifetime of hunting them I've learned to explore specific words down to their finest reduction, and in doing so have realized the limits of human language. Once these shortcomings are known, it follows that we're reduced ourselves, and when that denominator is finally reached a welter of kinship opens up in this world.

My father and I don't shoot many. We're marginal shots and don't hunt with dogs, but that's only part of it. The truth is hunters as a whole don't feed themselves well pursuing these creatures. While it's common to limit out on pheasants, ducks, doves, or quail, even a great shot with high-end dogs doesn't go home with many grouse. Their habitat certainly limits success, as do their numbers. Grouse hunting entails hacking through brush, crawling under windfalls, and getting hung up in briars, whereas most other game birds are flushed over fields or water. Dogs provide an advantage, but even then most grouse shots are taken with various limbs and trunks in the way. Other birds tend to flock or covey up as well, but grouse are often solitary, and even when a clutch is jumped they tend to scatter, spiraling off through the brambles. These traits combine to make taking one a notable feat. Tangled covers and a solitary nature, however, are only half of it. They reason, these birds, and combined with other factors, this intelligence buttresses the tools they need to survive. It's something all animals possess to some degree, but I'd never known that prior to hunting.

I'm unfond of the word instinct. It has its own validity, but like many words it's over-used, sapping its effectiveness. We use one word when we should use another, an error limiting our horizons. Any savvy, therefore, attributed to animals, any guile or methodology, is nearly always defined as instinct. This goes for fish, birds, insects, and mammals—anything. Pacific salmon, for instance, at finger-length, leave their birth waters then return after a life in the ocean. We call this instinct, backed by theories of sensual imprinting. Intelligence, though, never enters the debate. Birds, too, navigate hemispheres twice annually, and our hypotheses range from acute hearing to star mapping. While all this is probably true, we blanket the assumptions with "instinct," never pondering whether birds are simply smart. Canadian scientists recently proved the Rufus Hummingbird capable of episodic reasoning, or the ability to remember where it's been, when it was there, and why—a trait previously ascribed only to humans. Instinct, then, may have finally crested, and the animal kingdom might soon be accredited with more than gut reaction. It's here, though, where empiricism can lag. Lay intuition—human instinct, ironically—will tell you what you need to know most of the time and, for this, hunting certainly provides open access.

This bird wasn't telling me anything I didn't know. For years I'd known grouse could think. We'd pushed too many through countless covers only to have them thwart us with a move we hadn't anticipated. Still, even with the knowledge that people aren't the only reasoning beings, that can be hard to remember. We certainly appear to be the most intellectual creature on earth, and it's easy to slip back and think we stand alone, brotherless in an instinctual world. By the second flush, though, I'd been reminded.

For an hour or more we'd pushed the apple, birch, and hackberry beneath the mixed hardwood. The cover slopes down about a mile to a mountain stream. The mountain itself is called Jacob's Ladder, the highest peak in the valley. From the top of it fifty miles of Pennsylvania's hilltops lay in view. Days of broken cloud cover are best, when sunlight reaches through the holes like fingers to touch the valley below. Someone recognized this long ago and gave the place its name. It was a favorite of ours, and we often spent half a day covering it, enjoying both its museum of memories and the chance to generate new ones.

Hunters have an advantage. Anyone can intuit animal reason, but hunters set their wits against other creatures and are more able to see intelligence in that interplay. Most casual observers who flush a grouse, then, don't bother to follow where it goes or reason why it went there. They won't try to get it up again, either, studying behavior. Hunters do this by compulsion, and after time the word 'instinct' simply evaporates. This isn't something you see on first flushes. You're not ready and the sudden thunderclap of wings finds you scrambling. Either you shoot or you don't, but by that time you've recovered, usually getting a good line on where the bird went. Now you can deliberate. As you near the mark—a lone hemlock maybe, a fruit-heavy thorn apple—you've calculated where it is and how it'll behave. In other words, you're thinking, and each time you hunt a specific cover your ability to predict behavior becomes sharper. Rarely, then, are you far off your mark or unsure of what broad line of action the bird will take. It's the subtleties, though, that you don't foresee, and anything capable of subtlety is at least tinted by intelligence.

We first flushed it heading down the slope. We were spread our accustomed thirty yards apart and it got up between us. Neither of us saw it, but we followed the wing beats. Fall rains had been heavy and already we could hear the creek, knowing the bird was somewhere high in the strip of hemlocks lining a ridge that drops to the stream. People who don't hunt them would be amazed how often hunters don't see a flushed grouse. This isn't a result of distance. It's common for them to take off right in front of you, or just overhead, where you might never catch a glimpse. Again, the thick cover has something to do with it, but over time you understand that the bird plays the larger role.

As we neared the hemlocks we broke into our usual formation—one of us inside the trees, the other on the edge, hoping for an open shot. I had the lower line so wheeled around and entered the evergreens. My job was to flush. We knew it was in the hemlocks, just not where. It would be nervous, and in the thick canopy it would hold tight. I walked ten yards then stopped. They're jumpy when they can't hear you. Staring up, I started forward. After a few stops, I looked to my right, where I could see my father's orange vest moving through the brush

47

outside. You wait a moment, then continue. Two hemlocks stood before me, one with a split trunk and the other on a lean. Their lower branches intertwined and I bent down, placing a hand on the needled floor. Straight above, the grouse flew. I reared up into the dry, stiff limbs, cracking one off with an errant shoulder. I looked up. Only a shadowed form, far off in the tree tops, showed itself, while out in the berry and birch, my father never saw it.

The first few times you think it's coincidence. When you grouse hunt you bend down frequently. Unseasoned hunters, then, wouldn't have any reason to believe that a bird flushing at that moment was anything but chance—good luck for the bird, bad luck for the hunter. Years, though, teach. Grouse watch. They know they're hidden and observe hunters' movements from there. At one point I must have stared right at that bird. It waited, secure in its camouflage. When I ducked, it flew, careful to stay in the hemlocks to avoid my father. Once or twice like this you can dismiss, even a dozen times, but over years repetition is too much, and before I caught sight of that bird I remembered I was pursuing thought.

Organisms, though, come with limitations, and with grouse it's distance. They're built for bursts, not endurance, and their preference—particularly while the cover holds—is to settle down within a hundred yards of where they were flushed. As such, we were only half way through the hemlocks and knew where that bird would be. Still, it's tricky. Even when you know the exact location you can never be sure. Nearing where the hemlocks ended, I looked left off the steep drop to the creek.

My father pinched in, knowing the bird would hold tight. I stopped. I'd reached the last of the tall trees and stood a while, scanning the upper branches. Thirty seconds. Outside, fifteen yards away, my father stood too, eyes to the tree tops. I looked at him, then we shrugged our shoulders and lowered our guns. Twenty yards back, from a tree I'd walked by not long ago, the grouse flushed once more. Blocked by the fanned canopy, I never saw it. My father, surprised, turned and shot twice, but by that time the bird was far up the slope. We looked at each other and smiled, knowing we'd been bettered.

Fourth flushes are rare. By that time birds are sufficiently spooked and fly a greater distance. Places like Jacob's Ladder, though, can be different. Within vast habitat birds can be put up four, even five times. By its last trajectory my father knew this bird had flown far, but also knew that a hayfield ended the cover abruptly just a half-mile away. With that much room the bird would never cross open space. We pushed uphill, working to cover the abundant thorn apple and birch crowding the slope. A springlet seeps down the mountain here, and we took our usual positions twenty yards to either side, zig-zagging and stopping, hoping to put up another bird along the way. Soon the field was visible, where the woods made a right angle into the timothy. The grass was tall but dead, and through the thick growth we could see the field's dull gold both ahead and to the left of us.

When we came within fifty yards, where the slumping stone wall runs just inside the tree line, we nodded to one another, knowing the bird could fly at any moment. The cover here thins to hardwood, mainly oak and beech. A lone apple, old and sprawling, grows just off the tip of the angle out in the field. I was on the left, pushing inside the wood line, while my father moved through heavier timber. He reached the wall and stopped, then edged toward me. Soon we stood together, only yards from the apple and the end of the hunt. It's understood that luck is needed to get more than three flushes, and we weren't disappointed when we crossed the wood line to the left of the apple tree, to walk up through the field. My dad was to my right and when we came alongside the apple we both moved to shoot.

The grouse we get come two ways—luck and persistence. We hound birds as long as we can so flush more than usual, and if you shoot enough, eventually a few will fall. With my father right in front of me I never raised the gun. The grouse had been on the ground and took off low, keeping the apple trunk between us and itself. It stayed down, just outside the wall, level with the highest piece of shale. My father, off-balance, fell back a step and snapped a one-armed shot. Forty yards away the bird tumbled. We ran, scrambling along the wall, unmindful of whatever brambles we tore through. Reaching the mark, we looked down. A pair of breast feathers lay atop the stiff, bronzed oak leaves, and we heard a welcome sound. Feet away, nearly touching the wall, the dying bird pumped its wings in reflexive succession. I walked over and picked it up.

It's in the eye. You've followed these birds over half your life, hunting and observing. Each time, in different ways, they show you their layered intellect. When you knock one down, hold it in your hands, feel its life-thirst drain away, you look in its eye and know that much of what we mean by 'instinct' is bunk. On the wing, grouse are nearly an evanescence, an entity whose existence you can't be sure of. You chase them and chase them, and even when you get a good look it still seems like you're pursuing shadow. Rarely, then, do you touch one, but when you do all the uncertainty subsides. The bird is in your hands now, throbbing and warm, and this particular one had done all it could. Each time it flushed, the grouse deliberately kept as many objects between itself and its pursuers, and it chose angles—high and low—that gave it the best chance to live. It even used landscape, having on the final turn blocked us with the ridgeline and wall. The stones, though, weren't quite high enough, and an aimless shot brought it down. I gripped it. The wings finally pulsed to a stop and I lifted the head. Tissue covered half the eye, but I could see enough. Intricate and calculating, a brown pupil encased in burnt custard, this eye didn't seem much different than my own. For a fading moment life laid within it and I could see intelligence taking its last look on the world.

Grouse are like everything else. I know that now. From evident examples such as a wolf roaming the northern tiers to creatures like mussels—dedicated for eons to their private, successful lives in the brine—a common cognizance runs through all of us. You see this when you look for it, and when you find it, all being edges a little more in on itself. In the process, certain of our words merge, too, and terms like instinct and sentient become feeble, just as our own image of ourselves becomes both a lesser and greater thing all at once. We're knocked off the throne we too often place ourselves upon, but in the overthrow come to know a far deeper affinity with the world than we had before. I handed the bird to my father. He slipped it in his game pocket and we emptied our guns. Walking through the field we didn't say anything of consequence. What do you say? We simply moved in the tall grass—solemn, diluted, content.

IF TIME IN THE WOODS teaches you about other animals, if it teaches you about God—or at least forces confrontation with belief—it also drives you deep into far more intricate matter: you and how you relate to the people you love, caverns most of us consider scarcely navigable.

For me, trapping heightens everything, from correlation with nature to how far in it pulls the metaphysical fiber that so many seek from time outside. I'm not alone. I knew a guy in Alaska, a wildlife biologist out of Juneau for whom I occasionally worked. He'd grown up on a Minnesota farm, a life given to trapping. Through his job and his studies he knew nature thoroughly—from wolves and moose to voles and marmots—but attributed a more intestinal knowledge to trapping, along with his natural-world adoration.

"I can't explain it," he said, echoing Carl Wainwright's

unsteady assertion. "No one can. We all love the animals, spend tons of time studying them, but that's all bound up in killing them. Hunting and fishing are the same, I guess, but nearly every trapper does all three, and I've never met one who wouldn't say that hunting and fishing are second-rate, just something to do in the off-season."

He went on to say that no one who doesn't trap could ever understand the fervent compulsion it engenders beyond the fresh air and meager paychecks made from selling furs, partially because—as he said—no trapper can articulate it. My father and I are certainly among these, people for whom trapping's visceral appeal renders them dumb. But one piece I can at least fumble through is what it did for my relationship with him. This is true in numberless ways, but particularly so both in weathering adolescence and in understanding how different our upbringings were despite their many similarities.

One Pennsylvania farm we trapped covered a square mile. A former beaver complex converted to hay and irrigation ditches, its lack of tree cover occasionally led to some tough weather days, including the season I turned fifteen.

Most times, below zero at least meant high pressure, but not that year, at least not in late December. Rather than sun and no wind, the snow tornadoes whisked through the stubbled hay fields checkered between each water channel, snatching what flakes they could while gathering mass through the sheared crop. Nearly all nine inches that had fallen three nights before had been stripped, compiled in blue lips all along each west-facing slough bank. Though we still had two dozen traps here, spreading from the wooded upper Starrucca to the three farmer-channeled rivulets, the iced creek and the drifts in these irrigation routes had made for a long, unavailing morning.

Walking up the third channel's bank, frozen slush gummed our wader boots and we stopped every few strides to knock it loose. My pop used a long-handled trowel, while I carried the hatchet needed to free-up iced traps. The final set guarded this jump-across slough's mainspring, two-hundred yards from those we'd just checked, all of it wind-bitten open ground.

We'd come up the day after Christmas, and though we'd caught a dozen 'rats, when the weather turned animal activity dropped. Now, on New Year's Eve, with most of our sets made useless by the sudden freeze, we had mostly chopped ice for the last two days.

Snow blast had iced my pop's glasses over, and at such times I walked ahead, providing him movement to train upon. Our right cheeks received the wind and drift, and having started shaving months before, I now felt something new— ice veneering the days-old stubble that, in previous years, smoother skin would have melted.

Ten yards from where the slough simply appears in the hay I raised my eyes. The guide sticks used to funnel animals into the body-gripping trap were gone, knocked aside in the ever-verdant watercress. Cold in summer and warm in winter, the water here mostly never freezes, giving us a chance, and though my pop couldn't see, as we approached the pool my anticipation compiled.

"The trap's gone," I said, stepping forward, sinking hip-deep in drifts.

My dad joined me, and we stood either side of where the trap had been.

We enjoyed muskrat trapping, but mink were our chief aim, though we hadn't caught one since three years before, the first night we trapped Pennsylvania. Missing traps such as this elicited great excitement for the mink we hoped would be there, but by now such expectation had been largely throttled.

Still, hope is redoubtable. Within a couple of feet my pop's vision is fine, and bracing against the corkscrewed wind gusts, he bent down, finding the stake to which he'd wired the trap. More claw now than serviceable appendage, his hand hooked the wire and pulled, raising what looked like a snow island atop the watercress. White clumps sloughed off a muskrat's cinnamon guard hairs, and tapping loose a final tuft my dad looked over.

"Next time," he said.

We smiled, warmly, a rare island in itself going back to this time last year.

It may be true, I don't know, but I've heard that one of the oldest known writings comes from Sumatra, a clay shard upon which some words remain. Translated, they read:

Father: What were you doing last night?

Son: Nothing.

Father: Why did it take so long?

If it's not true, it may as well be. As my own father once said, every son since Adam wakes up one morning wondering who the dolt is he worshipped only yesterday, and it happens that fast.

"Enjoy it while you can," he said a couple of decades later to a cousin beaming over a son's birth. "You go from icon to ass overnight."

Whether wrought through endemic weaning rites, a teenager's self-inflation, generational discrepancies, or all three, such rifts are as inevitable as shaving, and surviving them, as I'd later learn, is contingent upon all that goes before. If every such friction is the same, though, they're likewise different, and in that regard my father and I had grossly varied childhoods.

If I'd only listened to my dad I wouldn't have learned much about my grandfather, certainly nothing vital. Though my pop has opened up a bit in his dotage, it's been modestly so, and while growing up I didn't quite have the ear yet to divine the gloom beneath the mirth. As far as I knew my dad's father was a funny, well-liked guy who enjoyed hunting and fishing and, in particular, the conviviality that followed. He drank, but I was too young to understand excess, let alone the Verdunscape that booze-bags wreak on their own families. In my teens, however, my mom began the corrective.

"You were fourteen when Fuddsy died, and you met him what, two, maybe three times? That wasn't an accident."

Born Owen Osborne Freeman, a drunken slur combined with a certain hat prompted his friends to dub him Fuddsy, after the Looney Tunes icon. Such tags usually imply someone well-regarded, and beyond his own walls my grandfather was just that.

"It's true," my mom said. "People liked him. He somehow kept his job through it all, and had a terrific sense of humor. You have to watch that though. A lot of alcoholics are funny, or at least sarcastic, but that can darken, and in the mean ones the families take it in the teeth. If nothing else, drunks require a lot of upkeep, and that wears you down."

It was all in my father's tellings, but I only heard the humor. His dad belonged to a Poconos fishing club that deeded some miles of the Tobyhanna River, condensing the name to "The Dream Mile," to which they often went from their Rydal, Pennsylvania, home on Philadelphia's Main Line. He masked a couple of drinking buddies as fishing partners, the most charismatic of whom was Gus, a tall, sprawling man with a jellied frame. Somewhere along the Tobyhanna's wooded confines Gus once slipped in a trout pool, taking an unscheduled swim. In his besottedness he stripped naked, then stumbled through the trees toward the lodge. He came on my grandfather, sipping a flask on the bank while my young dad and a couple of other guys fished a deep hole. Panting himself to equilibrium, the naked man leaned on a tree, wiping a few tresses of hair-snagged algae off his head.

"Jesus Christ, Gus," my grandfather said. "Who the hell are you? King Lear?"

Levity veiled even less of other tales.

"I learned how to drive young" my dad told me. "Maybe thirteen. Pennsylvania's the Quaker State, so has lots of Blue Laws, and I think even today you can't serve alcohol on Sunday. At any rate, you certainly couldn't then, and every breakfast at the Two Sisters Inn my dad would argue with the staff. He wanted a Bloody Mary, but they refused, and he'd always say, 'Oh for Christ's sake, just give me a beer then.' A lot of Saturday nights, though, spilled into Sunday, and one time he and Gus and some of the others were still tuned up by morning. When it was time to leave I came back from fishing and found him passed out. I lugged him to the car, stuffed him in the back, then did the best I could at the wheel. I'd practiced a bit, knowing this day was coming, but still had to stretch for the clutch."

As in most things, experience alone provides understanding. Somewhere in my teens I challenged my mom once, though not for long, saying Fuddsy just sounded like a good-timing guy.

"You hear well," she said. "But you don't listen. I didn't either, but I have the advantage. I knew the guy."

Though far less than most people, my mother was certainly conscious of her standing, and when my dad hadn't introduced her to his father after a year of dating she let him know it.

"Your dad wouldn't know how to lie if you gave him instructions," she said, "but I didn't know that then. He told me his dad wasn't terribly pleasant to be around, but after a year I just assumed it was me, that he was embarrassed to have me meet him."

One night after a date my dad thought his father was away,

but seeing the car out front he pulled a three-point turn. My mom stopped him.

"We do this now," she said.

My dad reversed, then put his arm over the seat while backing up.

"Fair enough. You want to meet him? Let's meet him."

"I'd never seen you're dad like that," my mom told me. "He wasn't mad, just resigned, and I knew before we went in that I wasn't going to see what I thought I was going to see, and that's how it played out."

It could have been scripted. When they opened the side entrance to the laundry room, there he was, on the floor.

"I thought he was having a stroke," my mom said. "His motor skills were shot and he was sitting down, propped on the inner door jamb, mumbling. 'Well, that's him,' your dad said. By the time we got to the car I could barely speak, and just said 'I'm sorry.' "

Before my mom met my grandfather, she had sympathy for alcoholics, a sentiment she tried but failed to retain.

"That flushes right out when you see what a drunk does to someone you love," she said. "It wasn't just the slovenliness. Your dad had a great guy in our wedding party, a college friend who was Jewish and, having grown up when we did, was quite sensitive about it. Somehow I was slated with Fuddsy to pick up several people at the train, Terry included. Your dad begged him not to say anything, and Fuddsy of course promised he wouldn't. Once everybody was in and we were on the road, though, your granddad—already a few belts in—looked over the backseat right at Terry and said, 'So, Matt didn't tell me any Hebe's were invited.' "

My dad had his own narratives, including those of attending the condition's untoward practicalities. Like many of the afflicted, my grandfather scoffed at Alcoholics Anonymous, and in the '50s the notion of dependency as a disease was inchoate, leaving asylums as the chosen refuge for drying-out drunks.

"It got so we barely needed to sign the paperwork," my dad said. "I just dropped him off when his body literally couldn't take another drop, and after a couple of days would pick him up. It was a real nut house too. There was an honest-to-God guy there who thought he was Napoleon, hand in the shirt and everything."

My grandfather had blown out a knee during his freshman year at Yale, forcing him out of football, and he repeatedly used that as one of many drinking excuses. When he was too far gone to be coherent he often mumbled the same thing, and "Set my leg, Coach" was a standard.

"One night I had him in a fireman's carry," my dad said, "over my shoulders, and when they opened the door and we walked in, Napoleon cocked an eyebrow and said, 'Ah, Josephine, the Coach is back.' "

My mom often told similar stories, but left in the bite.

"I was pregnant with you when your grandmother called once. She was dying of lung cancer and didn't have the energy or interest to manage Fuddsy. We found coverage for the girls and went over. Your grandparents belonged to an Episcopal church, and your dad's dad had charmed the priest enough to always take his side."

Paul, the clergyman, was there that time, half-holding my granddad up when my parents came in, trying to wipe vomit off his hands. My mom went to check on Kitty, my grandmother, but stayed long enough to see my dad take care of his father.

"Your father was a grown man by then," she said, "and he just walked over and flipped Fuddsy up on his shoulder. Paul, whom your dad liked, protested, but while he hardly ever gets it, this time your dad got that look. 'I'll tell you what, Paul,' he said, 'I'll handle the body. You take the soul,' then walked out and took his dad to the asylum."

Even today, with his father thirty years gone, my dad has only dabbled in the considerable scarring that Fuddsy inflicted on him. One of those forays, however, went deeper, revealing what allowed my father the distance he'd need to live a happier life than many children of alcoholics do.

"It was just another day really, but for me the pivot. On a night before we went up to The Dream Mile he'd been up to the usual stuff, though with a few more outrages than normal, saying nasty things, bullying my mother, things like that. On the drive up I made him swear it was over, that he wouldn't drink anymore, the same crap that families make drunks swear over and again, only I was young, ten I think, and hadn't learned. He didn't drink at the lodge that night, but of course the next day on the river I went looking for him and found his hip boots first, with a near empty fifth of whiskey inside one of them. I smashed it against a tree then sat for a bit before looking for him. That's it, I thought. I'm alone. I'd put my head down until I turned eighteen and that would be all, and for the most part it was."

Long before, my mother had told me that kids who grow up like that either go one way or another—dead in the footsteps or dead the other way. Fortunately, my dad went the other way, something never quite lost on me even in the depths of adolescence.

THERE'S NO SUCH THING as bad weather, Norwegians say, just bad clothing. The moment he had a son my pop knew the weather would eventually turn, inciting preparation, so that by the time it did sour he had the proper clothes. Still, prepared or not, eventually you just hunker and brace, hoping everything holds.

I had no antagonisms. No booze or abuse, no privations of any kind, simply the ubiquitous, on-schedule, as-yet-not-fully-fathomed rufflings between fathers and sons. It could be that he just got lucky, I don't know, but my dad did two things right. First, he ensured those rufflings went one way. If sleeping dogs should be left to lie, brooding teenagers should be left to brood. Second— as both precursor and backbone to the first—he sought ways to manufacture stability. Churches don't need to be built on rock, but they do need something solid, and from birth forward my pop staked out that solidity. All it takes is time, time and even a single shared interest.

"Find something you both like," he told me when Karen delivered Shannon. "Anything, and stick with it. Otherwise you're just punching a clock."

Fortunately, my dad and I had more than a few shared interests. We were a football family, for one, with all five of us watching pro games together every Sunday. To a lesser extent this went for baseball as well. By the time I was old enough to play, moreover, my dad coached both, keeping us tight. Mostly, though, it was the woods. Both of us have an inherent attraction to nature, and by the time I was an adult I realized that my father had probably used that innate interest as a sanctuary from his own dad, losing himself in field guides when he wasn't in the actual forest. When he had children of his own, that knowledge awaited bestowal, and I drank him up.

Fishing started our woods habits, but with my pop the experience was pervasive, making trout and bass incidental. Once, early on, we fly-fished one of the Starrucca's heavily-stocked stretches, casting near shoulder-to-shoulder with farmers and guys from Scranton plunking worms. Mid-April clammed the leafless banks, and my dad motioned me to the side.

"Let's sit," he said, nestling onto a boulder. Unaware, I put a boot on an adjoining rock.

"Look, all around. You see these birds moving through? It's a black-throated blue warbler migration. There must be a hundred of them."

Still working out the differences between titmice and

house finches on our winter feeder, I'd have never noticed, but dizzying the young birch and willow growth were dozens of white-breasted, black-masked, otherwise slate-blue birds. On the opposite bank and right behind us, groups of three and four leap-frogged one another upstream, moving, as my dad had said, through.

"These guys are up from Cuba and the Caymans, that whole Caribbean archipelago. A few might drop off to nest here, but mostly they're heading for Maine and Vermont, Quebec, places like that. They breed in heavy forests, usually on mountainsides. These are looking for any insects they can find now, fattening up for the final push."

With the fishermen knee-deep out front, casting and re-baiting, occasionally netting a trout, we sat silent until the last bird vanished.

More often fish had nothing to do with it. A few years later, while walking an ephemeral stream well off a trail in our Connecticut neighborhood, a rattle of leaves and intermittent wing beats froze my dad.

"Don't move," he said.

A mountain laurel thicket pinched us between its lingering parasols and the dry creek bed, while a ruffed grouse, hobbling along the bank, made several attempts to fly downstream, semi-skipping between each failed wing flurry. When it had out-distanced us by twenty yards, it came back within five, then repeated. I'd heard my father describe such behavior enough to know the bird wasn't disoriented.

"That's it, Mike," he said. "That's the broken-wing act. She

67

has a brood in this laurel. They should be able to fly by now, but let's stop anyway. If we just stand they might show themselves."

Frustrated that we hadn't pursued her easy-meal theatrics, the hen, now across the creek, flared mottled breast feathers. She clucked to still-concealed chicks before floundering ten yards more. To our left, screened in laurel, the young panicked, hopping by one's and two's to dense branches until eight had arrayed. Cardinal-sized, each fledgling jiggled along its respective limb until they burst across us toward their mother. She let them pass, then followed, disappearing beyond a boulder-ridden knoll.

"That's something, isn't it?" my dad said. "Other birds do that too, but grouse are famous for it. Two weeks ago we'd have traced our steps backward. If they're just eggs or flightless chicks there's a good chance of crushing them. You'll get to know them a lot more this fall."

He was right. I'd turned twelve that winter, meaning I could hunt and trap. Come October, then, a lifelong memory river—sprung from all that fishing and walking as a child—received its dominant influxes.

Even a few hunts, a few days of trapping, lays memories in thick, and by the time I'd turned sixteen there were too many to go back on: Porcupines, quills splayed, balled in complacent defense. Bobcat tracks, padding across streams atop snow-covered logs, then snaking blackberry canes, pawing vole tunnels. Foxes, red and gray, streaking over roads. A water snake, coiled, the leopard frog lodged in its throat. The raccoon skeleton, gooed with rotting parchment, eye sockets fouled with porcupine spikes. Snowshoe hares, turned white, holding tight in a blowdown or fronting a glacial erratic, hoping camouflage is enough. An ermine, turned white too soon, vanishing and appearing along a stone wall, snowless ground all around. A grouse, dead for an hour, three inches of snow atop him, my father's fingers finally dusting off the right patch of ground. Walking out of swamps, creeks, ponds, lakes, often empty-handed, often not, three or four muskrats dangled from our grips. Mink tracks, mink scat, mink scent, always leading us forward. Dusks along the Delaware, slinging flies to rising trout, then just sitting, listening. The melancholic ovenbird calls, the scarlet splotches of rose-breasted grosbeaks. Coyotes howling, pileated woodpeckers cackling, kingfishers stooping, splashing, coming off empty, sometimes not, ospreys clenching twitching trout while we casted below, and everywhere the other birds, all of them, alive in the brush, up in the conifer crowns, migrating north, migrating south, nesting, gleaning, singing, always moving.

When it happened, then, it didn't have sufficient punch. I found the friends you're not supposed to find, and likely became one myself. Nights at home last year—watching baseball and football among family, reading—became nights abroad, drinking beer, whiskey, pretending I understood girls, all the templated nothing that passed teenaged Sumatran nights so long ago. By day I poached rabbits and squirrels with friends, gigged frogs, caught trout. By winter, junior year, I attended a class a day, maybe two. The camaraderie had something to do with it, but mostly I just slipped off alone and walked, then walked further. The Norwalk River ran across the street from Wilton High School, intermittently abutting a commuter line. My dad and I trapped it in many places, and I substituted most class time with treading the rails and river banks, looking. Come June, with a couple of F's marring a string of incompletes, my dad took his chance, and for the first time before or since directed that look my mother had described my way.

"You're going to prep school."

It's difficult to gauge what would have happened otherwise. While it's possible a baseline respect for hierarchy, for blood, would've blunted disaster, that's uncertain. As it was, too much experience, too much work and satisfaction, filled the short distance between us to allow for any other outcome.

"O.K.," I said, breaking most of the weather as fast as it had arrived. The moment's lack of tension didn't surprise me, for it had been subsiding by degrees for months, a decline initiated the previous fall while we hunched in front of the Pennsylvania cabin's conical fireplace.

MOST THANKSGIVINGS THE WEATHER was seasonal. Overcast, drizzly November days, often a touch of snow, thirty-some degrees. Other times we broke a sweat running traps, feeling odd in shirtsleeves. Still others saw the lake snap shut overnight, freezing creeks in oyster-shelved barrens, turning a five-hour trap line into eight while we chopped ice, moved sets, and slugged forth. If such weather slows muskrats, however, they remain somewhat active, and by the time I was sixteen we'd learned the cold. Summer scouting had turned up several warm water springs, and that season—a snow bunting year, the Arctic rim birds pushed down by only the bitterest winters—we'd caught thirty 'rats in the first three nights.

Success breeds work, which in trapping means skinning and stretching. Normally a joy, the searing cold can make fur handling a chore, as after a day afield it takes a couple of hours to loosen joints enough for maneuvering jackknives and manipulating hides. The high volume that year, combined with my floundering through the warps of adolescent cocksureness made the looming twenty-odd 'rat night that much more unattractive. Thank God, I thought, for fire, fire and football.

The cabin was just that—a small living space with a smaller kitchen and two scant bedrooms, with the living room fireplace—a cone of sheet metal—as trapping season's focal point. Thanksgiving, too, marks college football's rivalry week, which that year distilled any need for conversation down to spare punt-pass-kick commentary.

As predicted, the skinning took time. After fleshing two or three 'rats and then stretching hides over wire frames, we'd sit before the fire, massaging hands to gradually work out the numbness. That year had been compounded by snow, an otherwise welcome trap line addition, as most animals ramp up activity during precipitation, with snow having the added benefit of tipping which creatures have wandered through. On our line, then, it was common to find everything from otter to beaver to bobcat to coyote to fox tracks traversing various terrain. Mink were often among these, and that morning we'd had a scare, a frustrating one.

Charlie's Slough was one of our staples, a quarter-mile long spring-fed watercress gullet feeding the Starrucca. It never freezes unless beavers are present, and while they'd dammed it that year, it was far down, too far to think that what little backflow reached the headwaters would be affected. Two inches of snow had fallen the night before, though, after which the temperature re-dropped, and mink tracks dotted right over the frosted ice, skimming two traps we'd set among a hornbeam's exposed roots. As much as the age of sixteen had occluded everything else, it had only clarified my mink drive, and I was subsequently livid—livid that we'd missed a mink, livid at my father, and livid at not understanding why I was livid at my father.

That night, as one football game turned to the next, with just the odd "Nice stick" or "Jesus, catch the damned ball!" cutting the silence, the 'rat burden dwindled, and after several breaks before the blazing oak and maple our hands finally reinvigorated, making the last few skinnings a pleasure. Everything aside, it had been a terrific three days. In spite of the cold, thirty muskrats was our best take by far, and we'd coated on the usual layer of hunting memories, sprinkled with some seldom encountered birds—a brown creeper and red-breasted nuthatch pair among them, along with the red-shouldered hawk that morning at Charlie's, lifting off the ground just ahead, battering snow-drowsed limbs, a red squirrel limp in its talons.

Mulling it all before the fire, seated on the bench in front, I pressed the day's last numbness from my hands, staring at ember. Having hung the final 'rat pelt to dry, my father sat alongside, rubbing his own hands, both still sheened in blood. A touchdown, tie game, and my dad picked up a quartered log to jostle coals, then laid the piece on.

"We certainly had those traps in the right place," he said.

"Mm," I replied.

The new log caught, the splinters incinerating first. We

said nothing further, but if as a child my dad had once counted himself alone after smashing his old man's whiskey bottle against a tree, as a doubt-addled teenager I had a constitutionally different experience.

"My God," I thought, sitting next to him by fire. "I'm not alone."

In time the mink came, and did so reliably. After seven minkless years, we finally figured it out, averaging five a season in the week we trapped Pennsylvania. Still amateur status, but not embarrassing.

My last fall in college, one of those came from the lake before the cabin, along the undeveloped shore where we ended each day. The week was nearly up, one night to go, and compared to other years had been sultry—fifty degrees throughout, T-shirts by noon. Six mink pelts hung from the ceiling alongside the requisite 'rats, and we'd both shot a couple of grouse, enjoying them with mushrooms and sherry.

A month before, near the end of football season, the captains and coaches had been kind enough to give me a game ball, engraved with date and score. I played defensive tackle and had made enough plays that week for them to tip an already senior-friendly vote my way. Keeping the ball in my locker for a couple of weeks, I took it to the field after the last game. Calling my pop aside, I removed the ball from a paper bag.

"Here. Thank you."

He held it, reading the inscription, thumbing deep, cauterized grooves. Turning it over a couple of times, his eyes stayed down, watching fingers fiddle with laces. They lingered, then he looked up, nodding.

With the fine weather we'd pulled the canoe from storage, paddling across the lake rather than parking in the usual driveway closest to the sets. We trapped here more out of tradition than any expectation, as up to that time we were far more comfortable reading running water. Nevertheless, we'd seen tracks throughout the years here, and knew our knowledge was improving.

Two outlet sets—placed right where the Louisiana waterthrush had been—were empty, and shoving the bow into brush, we left the canoe to wade the shallow shore, checking each trap along the wooded edge. Combined with the overcast sky, the windless day reflected the maple and hemlock off the waters ahead, which felt like ours alone now that the cabins were winter-vacant.

Most traps we simply walked by, making no adjustments, but once or twice we dipped beneath sun-starved laurels for slight tweaks—scratching sand away to lower a trap, repositioning a guide stick. A hundred yards from the outlet our last set mirrored the others, a foot-gripper tight to a sanded-in rock. Twenty yards out we saw movement, a mink—large, dry, male—struggling with the yellow birch sapling he'd wrapped around. Caught by a back leg, he pawed away, stuck in place by the now slackless tangle of wire and chain.

"I'll be damned," my dad said, hustling forward.

Most animals drown. Things, though, go awry, and live

ones are taken. With mink, back leg catches combined with shallow water are common culprits. We'd wired to a log out in the lake, staking a dead hemlock branch in the sand for any animal to wrap up in, keeping it in water, but this guy had stayed landward. Judging by the mostly undisturbed bank, he was likely caught not long before we arrived.

Positioned on either side of him, we assumed an accustomed choreography. My pop distracted him with his trowel, while I snipped the ruined sapling with wire-cutters. I then grabbed the chain and waded shin-deep, dangling the now hissing mink before submerging him. Gripping his back legs, I held them above water, while my dad, using the trowel, pressed the neck to the sandy bottom. The small, black-pearl eyes stretched wide, and ivory teeth set in pink gaped a lake-muted valediction. The muscles slackened. The eyes rolled once, twice, before a lone bubble rose off the tongue and all went limp. I lifted the lithe, dripping form back to air, and tucking the trowel beneath an arm, my dad cradled the body in both palms, freeing it as I depressed the trap springs.

Wading ashore, he pressed water from dark, oiled fur. I remade the set and, still stooping beneath evergreen limbs, we turned, headed for the canoe, hearing the wing rush out front. Mergansers, fifty or more, lit in unison, rippling water. The males' white bodies and dark green heads looked like different species compared to the gray, rust-crested females, and if the hemlocks had screened us on approach, the birds now recognized potential trouble. Three males dropped off, aligning between us and the flock, grunting the rest outward.

Once clear of the limbs, we rose, and as we waded away they at last deemed us non-threatening. The lake is run-through with yellow perch, and the ducks stationed in rough parallel lines. Collaborative hunters, mergansers work in similar fashion to porpoises, diving low to cram schools toward one another, and as we reached the boat we looked back several times to watch fish slip down happy throats. I stood by the stern, steadying a gunnel, while my father, laying the mink in the middle, took a paddle and sat in the bow, awaiting the push toward deeper water.

The Germans have a concept called *heimat*. Derived from their word for "home," it's not necessarily that, but more exactly the place—tangible or not—where you're most at ease, where the world's prevailing imprint upon you is affinity, not provocation. It's most often an abstraction, or where specific actions in specific spaces quell life's concomitant devils. Playing piano, weeding peas, eating hot dogs at Fenway Park. Roping calves, stitching quilts, sculling the Chesapeake. Sucking fireballs in a penny arcade. Everyone's *heimat* is different, and there is no wrong answer. While I didn't know the term then, learning it later only buoyed with sound what I'd already felt, that whether paddling calm, warm water with a mink between us or bearing ice-danced winds on an unobstructed plain, my father and I had identical *heimats*, trapping the otherwise insignificant springs, streams, ponds, and lakeshores draining Pennsylvania's obscurest corner.

In keeping with what the Minnesota-farm-kid-turned-Alaskan-biologist told me years later, the moment my dad and I set our first trap on one of those Connecticut golf courses, trapping superseded hunting and nearly reduced fishing to memory. Still, grouse hunting remained a passion and, for me, ritual and what it fosters were indivisible from my devotion to it, something that might have been mistaken for a surrogate denomination but was merely fundamental to the conduit I preferred—the world outside.

Like so many in their generation, both my parents had attended church as kids, but then dropped it once they left their respective homes. Even though they had their own kids not long after, they never picked it up again, leaving the three of us to free-graze theologically, something both my mom and dad agreed was proper.

"It's cheating to have it pounded into you from the

cradle," my mom said one warm evening at the lake when I was around ten. "Go out there on your own, every day, and smell the air. You earn it more."

That same summer my dad and I were breaking down our fly rods as twilight shrouded the Delaware just across from Hancock, NY. This was long before *A River Runs Through It* had popularized fly fishing and, especially on Sundays, we always had a favorite stretch nearly to ourselves, except for an elderly man who drove up from New Jersey every weekend. Sitting on a rock cairn, watching trout nip insects in last light, he said after a lengthy silence, "Who needs church, eh?"

My dad smiled, and after we nodded goodbye and walked away, he said, "Fishermen say that a lot, or at least claim that 'The river's my church,' but that doesn't make it any less true. Rivers are there all the time, the woods too, and we come to them to think."

If I've never attended a church service, then, I affiliate through ritual. The timely, consistent performance of acts—anything from spring cleaning to an annual camping trip to vespers—frees the mind in important ways. Repetition allows contemplative latitude, where a minimum of intellectual energy is expended on the task at hand, emancipating the remainder to snare what it can. It's like drifting a net on the high seas. Most days nothing of worth is caught. Through maintenance, however, by mindlessly working the net free of rubbish, once in a great while you harvest a fish. The catch itself comes seemingly as an afterthought, an ancillary boon of the persistence that produced it, but the meat it grants is flesh to be savored. This makes ritual the habitat of theology, a place where an individual goes to encounter the divine, to sense—if never touch or see—the supernatural. If ten thousand years of religious evolution have fostered great animosity among differing peoples, it has also taught us the ability of ritual to bring the mind in as close a contact with God as humanity can come, or even bear. From Jews to Muslims to Christians to Hindus, all sects of all structured houses have their own liturgical methods in the hope of inspiration. Other people, of course, do too, for churches aren't the only places to practice repetition, and far from the lone access to ritual's considerable well-spring. Prior to having my own child, then, for thirty years I maintained part of my own private inquiry through hunting grouse with my father.

It's not that we hunted to specifically dwell on God. Far from it. Our annual pursuits of grouse were certainly similar, however, to the ritual of church attendance for what may be a majority of devotees. On any Sabbath, in any venue, a plurality of the congregation is likely there more out of habit or social conscience than a desire to commune with any deity. Regardless, at least some of these people some of the time—through adherence to the rituals practiced within—find their holy moments scattered about this cradle of procedure. Enwrapped in automated iteration, they brush up against the ether, when the mind is most free of distraction and where spirituality is so often piqued. Though I relish the woods for countless reasons, it's probably this same vulnerability—the erratic exposure to teleology that people find in church—that above all others keeps me going back there. That was certainly true of trapping and hunting, particularly with my dad, experiences which built on those incipient inklings I'd had while swimming Smiley Slater's stretch of the Starrucca long ago.

Most of us maintain some vestigial connection with land and the rituals practiced upon it. Some people, for instance, can't live without their gardens, even if only a herb pot on a downtown windowsill. Others have fly fishing, while others still their Saturday park walk. Hiking soothes some, while a few aerate themselves each season gathering mushrooms. It's a rare person, then, who doesn't sustain a repetitive reciprocity with land in some way, and though we've retained these rites for many reasons one remains prominent—by performing familiar acts upon familiar terrain the mind is nearly detached from what the body does and, as in all ritual, becomes more refined. It doesn't happen every day, or even every year, but in elusive, unscripted moments the specter of God can bump up against the human mind, leaving its impression for a lifetime of revisiting. The opposite, however, can happen, too. Rather than an afterlife a void is sensed, and with it the crippling sensation that nothing exists beyond this world. Repetition, then, opens the mind fully, leaving it as susceptible to disruption as it does to comfort.

My father and I had hunted the same covers for so long that even after a couple of seasons we scarcely needed to talk. Each of us knew at just which hemlock to stop, waiting for the other to wheel around so we could change direction, or when both of us needed to shade a little to the right or left, and at what angle, so we'd be sure to push this or that thorn apple stand, or maybe a certain rose tangle. When I was a school kid we drove from Connecticut to Pennsylvania all fall and winter to hunt. Once I went to prep school (and then on to college and beyond) that changed, confining us to the week around Thanksgiving, when we'd usually hunt an hour or two each afternoon once the traps had been checked. Still, our love of hunting never flagged, and we came to those covers like pilgrims, re-connecting with the land and each other while moving over ground so familiar that it seemed like our own skin, with the snarled apple trees and bent-back birch stands like additional organs, as vital as the rest. For as many covers as we hunted, though, the forest girding Coxton Lake was among the best, and if either of us were pressed to name a favorite hunt, it would be the three hours it took to circumnavigate the lake and everything that its surrounding ground offered.

The fall after I graduated college we were doing just that. I'd picked up a job painting houses but had been given the week off as the work transitioned from outdoors to indoors. I never asked either of my parents, but what appeared to be my directionless ambitions didn't seem to bother them. While it never occurred to me until Karen called to say she was pregnant, my ostensible career path from high school forward looked every bit like I'd never planned anything in my life, and professionally speaking that remains true. Fortunately, without ever discussing it with me, my parents seemed to know more than I did, that professional orthodoxy wouldn't be my calling, that mobility and a desire to quench something unquenchable were my drivers.

Days before she died when I was twenty-six, my mom pointed that out, saying it all came from her, that while she loved her life and her family, they had hobbled what had been a more restless spirit. She could hardly lift a hand at that point, but her eyes hadn't lost a thing, and more than implied the rest.

My dad, too, in his own way, seemed to encourage what he and my mom, either tacitly or not, agreed was my given path. He'd coached my peers in football from Pop Warner through senior year in high school, and after everyone graduated college many of them sought job references and connections in fields like marketing, advertising, and sales. He always acquiesced, prompting me to ask the same. He'd once collaborated with Carrier, the air-conditioning firm, and told me a friend of his could arrange an interview for a job servicing and installing home units. If I had been more sensitive, or hadn't spent so much time with him, I may have taken that as a slight, but to me it translated immediately as, "Business is no life for you. Go find out what is."

Some of us, then, get lucky. People with unconventional thirsts need flexible parents, and I certainly had those, never hearing a peep nor sensing a peep needed to be made as one odd job led to the next. In the meantime, such work served its purpose, sustaining me while I managed a rapidly accruing wanderlust, an agitation yet to be stilled that first year out of college.

At two-thousand feet above sea level, the lake can see weather on par with much of New England. Though the overcast sky on this day provided low pressure and a bit of insulation, it still had a nip, and the constant brush-beating kept our blood moving. Some of the best cover is right near the cabin. Aging apple trees, knotty and worn but still productive, rise out of raspberry thickets interspersed with aspen and jack pine. This secondary hodgepodge runs east for a half mile or more, until the growth thins to mature hardwoods near the lake's trickling outlet. Grouse come here to feed. A pair had flushed in near succession, exploding from beneath the fermenting fruit of a last apple tree. I shot and missed and they headed for the hemlocks bunched along the outlet, where my dad's pointing to that water-thrush remained as clearly etched as the paddle we'd shared just last fall with the dead mink lying between us. We knew the grouse would be there and without a word walked beneath the hardwoods, eyes forward to the conifers.

Grouse in hemlocks are a tough quarry. Perched high, the thick needles make seeing difficult, and often all you hear are percussing wings and a few dead needles fluttering to the ground. That's how it went with these. Moving many yards apart, our footfalls fell silent in the mulch. After a time we flushed one, then the other, but never saw a feather. Grouse, though, make a sonic rush that can be traced. They'd headed up along the lake, where a thin ribbon of hemlocks continues before ceding to beech and maple. Here the hunting concentrated. Short of ample snow or abnormal cold, grouse aren't usually found in hemlocks unless chased there, as the trees aren't a complete habitat and the hardwood just off the lakeshore is too sparse to provide security. Birds pushed out of the outlet hemlocks either settle in the ones further upshore or head through the hardwoods into the blackberry thickets on the lake's far side. Edging closer together, then, my dad and I moved forward, he in the deciduous stand, me in the hemlocks.

Hunting is peculiar. Birds were ahead of us and we knew it, yet having been through this cover for so many years and knowing their habits so well we knew approximately where they'd be. As such, our anxiety was completely nullified by familiarity and our minds left free to roam. The lake lay still, the water resting in silver and black bars depending on how the light hit. I walked and stopped, walked and stopped, each time looking to the high branches, waiting for a grouse to fly. Years before, one had burst from the wind-beaten laurel knit to the shore, and I now pressed into these spiny branches, hoping, again, to push one out. My father skirted the mesh of hard and softwoods, walking as I walked—pause, repeat, pause, repeat. After some time we reached the swell, where the hemlocks bulge into hardwoods.

Both of us were cloistered beneath the darker trees, knowing we were near the last of where a grouse might be. Out ahead, low, two hemlock branches knocked softly together and I strained to hear flushing wings. Nothing. I looked. Sometimes, as did that bird at Jacob's Ladder, grouse fly silent, dropping straight off a perch before pumping themselves forward. This was different. In front, directly between us, a barred owl flew, heading back toward the outlet. I never moved. Level with our own heads, the face was round, nearly human, with black eyes counter-sunk in stone-like arches. It looked straight at me. I listened for wing beats, a rush of air, anything. As it flew by, the feathers in both the wings and along the body were nearly countable. Layered seamlessly, they fit amongst themselves like marbled tile, complex pattern conjoined to complex pattern, each a centrifuge bound to its tangents. It was design, constructed, and it was perfect. I looked in its eyes once more and it in mine before it passed, then I watched its broad, long wings propel it beneath the boughs. I looked at my dad. He'd seen it too. He nodded his head and we pushed up through the rest of the cover, I on unsteady legs.

Design is the divide, the place where watersheds separate. If we believe life was created, or designed by an overseer, we tumble into one spillway. If we believe life simply happened, designed by chance, then we flow out with the other. Whichever way we've fallen, though, we generally come to peace with the rise and fall of our chosen waters. Even if comfortable with chance, most people weave at least a little of creation into themselves, some sense of relief that their personal identities and those of their friends won't be lost upon death. I've done this. Though I've not subscribed to any fixed religion, I share with those who have, sensing that a designing hand plays a part and that life is recycled, giving some sort of sustainability to each form. I take comfort in that, and though I still do, the sight of an owl—otherwise meaningless—knocked that stasis sideways.

That creature was designed. In that, at least, I'm secure. A gulf, however, exists between the design of chance and that of conscious intent, and in the brevity of a moment I saw in

those deep-set eyes and the silence of those wings the whit-
tling of time, the chiseled features of perfection that only
great ages and many failures had put together with neither
purpose nor cognizance. In the patterned intricacy of breast
feathers I sensed oblivion, the looming effacement of identity
paired with death, impacting with the same force that liminal
surges of immortality wrought through these same rituals have
produced before and since. It was a reversal of considerable
torque. Then as now I don't know what form of God awaits at
death or how, in fact, our souls pass on, only knowing that I
believe, but the memory of a barred owl, and the asphyxiating,
atheistic terror it engendered, always sends me scrambling for
that more comforting sanctuary, however abstract. If nothing
else, each time that bird's image recrudesces it reminds me of
why people as a whole affix themselves to both a God and an
afterlife. To not do so is to flirt with chaos on earth and annihilation beyond, a doubt-riddled abscess with a troubling half-life.

I'VE NEVER BEEN TO FLORIDA, though through memory graft I feel like an oblique native, at least of the long-buried Panhandle coast. Having spent World War II there as a kid, my father went back on business in his late thirties, three decades after leaving, and should I ever go I'd likely experience the same recoil, with the detail of what came before being that vivid.

"I couldn't believe it," he said. "It was all gone. Nothing but Winn Dixie's, KFC's, and miniature golf. One traffic light after another. Back then there was the base and not much else. A few clans out in the palmetto maybe, but mostly it was damned near frontier."

He lived there from the ages of four to eight, when most of us retain our first deep-tissue memories. In December 1941, his father was thirty-five with a gimpy knee and horrific eyesight. He was also flat drunk. Still, when the Japs pulled their voo-doo he shoved it all aside with everyone else. The Marines wouldn't take him, but the army—needing all roles filled—did, stationing him with the Eighth Air Force near Panama City, where he served out the war as Tyndall Field's athletic director.

Prior to Pearl Harbor, Panama City was mostly a sedative, a seaside escape for those nearby Alabamians who had managed to enrich themselves during the Civil War's protracted desolations. Beyond a few thousand permanent residents, though, the surrounding area was mostly swamp, fine ground for fetally-positioned airmen to rake machine guns all day, as Tyndall Field was the finishing school for ball turret gunners, the guys wadded up in the bellies of long-range bombers. Beyond training and the occasional leave in Panama City, however, there wasn't much to do, and the army—which governed the budding air force then—fostered cross-base athletic rivalries, providing my pop a bat-boy job.

The only family photo I'm aware he's kept still hangs in his office, where he and his older brother watch Ted Williams display a mock swing. Once, during another game, my dad stooped to fetch a forgotten bat in high grass. Usually people grasp the thin end, but here he grabbed the fat, back-pedaling apace after sighting the red-touch-yellow-kills-a-fellow coral snake coiled about the handle. Roughly a foot long, cobra-related corals aren't big enough to puncture most human body parts, but finger webbing is highly vulnerable, something my dad notes. "If I'd have picked that bat up where you normally do, neither me, nor you, nor your two sisters would be here."

When he wasn't bat-boying he spent nearly all his time in

the woods—out in the trees, deep in the swamps, plying the littoral—soaking up John Pittman.

Before I learned about any of it—the Middle Passage, slavery, Reconstruction, Jim Crow, lynching, Freedom Rides, the low-hum quotidian frictions that make up most of American racial life—I learned John Pittman. My dad didn't mention him as a principle influence until years later, but when I was a kid he didn't have to, for at both my urging and his eagerness he told and re-told stories of keeping Pittman's pace through Florida's unmarred wetlands, branding such memories into my own deep-tissue.

As an adult I once stood in a circle while a wedding progressed towards dinner. A relative asked my dad where his outdoor interests came from, and though I'd never asked him the same, by that time I could have verbatimed the answer.

"My father," he said. "He took me hunting and fishing, so that's certainly something I can credit to him. The other though, probably bigger, was a guy named John Pittman."

If my grandfather's age, Yale education, and lousy physical state combined to make him an officer in Florida, the segregated army was enough to cram most black soldiers into similar places, though at lower ranks. Pittman, then, was technically in the motor pool, tuning occasional engines, but mostly he and his wife were assigned to maintain both officers' quarters and personal lives. Subsequently, his wife Lily-Belle cooked and cleaned, while Pittman himself became a surrogate father to my pop.

"He and Lily-Belle didn't have kids yet," my dad said, "which was fine by me. I followed him everywhere. He'd grown up in Alabama—God knows where—but wherever it was he'd lived off the land. Maybe it was a function of the Depression, I don't know, but mostly I think he just came up that way. He ate everything. Alligators, rattlesnakes, possums, frogs, turtles, herbs, mushrooms, along with the usual stuff, rabbits and squirrels, things like that. He was lethal with a rifle. My dad would give him ten .22 shells, and he never came back with nine squirrels, always ten. He must have missed things once in a while, but I only remember it once. The dogs were swimming in the bay when a big gator came in, closer and closer. John ran to the cabins then back out to the end of the dock. The damned dogs thought the gator wanted to play. He ripped a few rounds off before it dove, but a .22 was the only gun not locked up, and he knew he had to go for the eyes. He just missed, and you could hear the bullets ricochet off that hide. Sometime later my brother and I were swimming there, and a cottonmouth ribboned right between us. You could count the scales, and every ounce of air went right out of me. If John had been there, that would've been one dead snake."

My dad breathed John Pittman, and in turn breathed him into me. The stories fell like rain. Through all of them Pittman doesn't say much, just moves. He likely spoke the garbled Deep South patois scarcely comprehensible to Northerners, whether off a white tongue or black. My grandfather had dragged a couple of bird dogs along from Philly, one of whose names—Target—made it into the transferred Pittman lexicon.

"He never said both their names, and for some reason made it sound like they were a pack, not just two. Feral hogs were everywhere, real nasty things, and my dad's dogs would tangle with them at night. John had rigged a flashlight to a rifle barrel, and when the dogs howled he'd come over to our quarters and ask for the gun. 'Sah,' he'd say. 'Tah'get an em is in behind da hawgs a'gin.' Soon enough we'd hear a shot, maybe two. That usually meant as many dead hogs, which John would dress and cure. Lily cooked it all."

Occasionally she cooked rattlesnake, plucked right outside the cabins' front doors.

"I guess they felt more heat next to the walls, but in the morning there were always a couple of diamondbacks asleep on the porch, sometimes more. They couldn't really move until the sun warmed them, and one of Lily-Belle's jobs was to come by early and sweep them off. Sometimes she did more than that. They looked like fire hoses. John was tall, maybe six feet, and when he held a dead one up by the rattles the head as often scraped the ground."

Fishing, too, was prominent, catfish and bluegills—bream in South-speak—along with whatever they filched from the surf. One such ocean foray came a couple of days after an early-season hurricane flirtation, leaving a horrific wrack of tree trunks and heaped kelp, shrimp nets and busted crab pots.

"There was a picture of my mother on that beach, taken from an angle where you could look down the tree line a few miles. Nothing was there, just palms. We gave up fishing before we started, and John spent the day scavenging flotsam. Near the trees he spotted something while trying to unravel a gillnet from driftwood. A snapping turtle was making its way back to the swamps, maybe after laying eggs, I don't know, but I was five, maybe six, and it looked like a Buick. At any rate, it didn't live long. There was trash all over the beach, and John found a length of stovepipe wire. He made some kind of noose, then slipped it around the turtle's neck. He had me hold the tail while he pulled the wire with one hand and unsheathed his machete with the other. One whack, that was it. The white sand just sucked up all that blood. He picked up the wire, dangling the head, and I reached out. His hand shot from nowhere and grabbed my forearm, right here. 'Watch,' he said, then put a stick as thick as a broom handle by the mouth. The head snapped it in two. 'Das why ya nevah put ya hands nay'um,' he said. He tied a rope to the tail and hung it up while we continued combing, then carried it home hours later and had me help him cut it up. Philadelphians love snapper stew, especially on the Main Line, but no one would it eat if they saw one butchered. The stench would make a combat medic puke."

Maybe it was because he spoke so infrequently, at least through my pop's tellings, but after a while I imagined little more than Pittman's hands. Hands are the agents. Our brains might make us what we are, but hands are the instruments, executors of nearly every cerebral mandate. When we learn, then, particularly when young, we most often do it by watching someone's hands.

As such, whatever my father said when he first laid a muskrat out to skin is lost, but I still see his fingers, his thumbs, his palms and veins, slipping the blade in one hind Achilles then the next, slitting it round. From those cuts up it went, up the shin equivalent, up the thigh, joining the other, making a slice from heel-to-crotch-to-heel, then two more slits round the front ankles. Beyond that there was pulling, sliding that hide off like a sweater, only cutting again around the ears, the eyes. A final slice took the nose, whiskers too, and that was it, an inverted pelt ready to stretch. If I was watching my father's hands, I may as well have watched John Pittman's, shaking all those rabbits and squirrels out in Florida's long-forgotten swamps, coming away with the same sweet-sticky residue that coated my pop's palms, then my own, dropping off in maroon flakes. As a teen, too, I killed a dozen snapping turtles, maybe more, hooking them on trotlines, cubing meat and making stew. I never had to look up how to dress one. Through the beheadings and the hangings, all the blood and all the viscera, I simply conjured those deft Southern hands.

Hands are how we know we're in the world, in the world and not alone. Though other senses might be lost, adjustments can be made, but if you lose touch you lose it all. Not long after college and just before my mom died, I took a job installing invisible fencing, the shock-collar pet containment systems. It was solid work, and after a year as an installer and pet trainer stationed in Connecticut, they moved me to Vermont, where I inherited a problem Chow. The dog continually ran through the unseen border. Such cases involved explaining certain collar manipulations or training tweaks, and the wife often invited me into the kitchen for these sessions.

By chance she was from Alabama as well, though I never asked how she wound up in New England. A mother of five, her four oldest kids were always in school, with the youngest, maybe seven and severely disabled, her constant charge. With all else spindled in a framed body brace, the child's head lolled to the side while all four limbs lay limp from her suspended body. Though her eyes blinked and occasionally roamed, she most often looked like a hypothermia victim, and other than a steady, wheezy aspiration, never made a sound except once.

Sitting across from her mother while boosting the collar's shock strength, I saw the girl rear her head a few inches before issuing a low, static moan. Her mom broke off our conversation, turning to slip a hand around her daughter's own, massaging it with her thumb and forefinger. In seconds the child quieted, relaxing her head, and the woman turned back.

"Touch is everything," she said, continuing to hold her daughter's hand until I'd finished.

I've managed John Pittman as best I can. In the beginning, when the stories still rolled, there was nothing to manage. I simply wallowed in the lore, the detail, in everything John had translated to my dad and he in turn redistributed to me. History, though, as history does, eventually oxidized that chastity.

Early in life I asked my dad about our family tree. "Don't shake those things too hard," he'd said. "A lot of fruits and nuts fall out." Beyond his father, then, I know little, but learned from a cousin that along with Puritan stock we had some Southern heritage.

"Mill-associated people," he said. "The Carolinas I think, a daughter of whom married into the Philly lineage."

Whether these were antebellum true-bloods or carpetbaggers I don't know, but it hardly matters, for John Pittman was likely born around World War I, into deep-woods, Yankee-hating, nigger-hanging Alabama. Rather than any function of the Depression, then, or affection for the lifestyle, Pittman's family probably havened themselves in the region's remotest outback, where living off the land was the wage of comparative peace. Still, it's near certain that the Terror found them, and these were people for whom cantering hooves and rattling Tin Lizzies—wild screams piercing either—breached more than the ever-Confederate night. That wasn't my time and it wasn't my terrain, and as I've aged I've striven to judge the acts, not the actors. Besides—Eve, evolution, or otherwise—I believe in original sin, in the dank, base denominator governing our most deeply-interred, tinder-packed precincts, and I've lived long enough now to know better. Had that been my time, had that been my terrain, it would have taken strength that I'm not sure I possess to have not joined the others atop those cantering hooves, screaming wildly. I scarcely understand myself, then, let alone the world, so only shuffle along, hands on high for the grasp, the palms, just a fingertip, of those coquettish better angels.

More than a few times I've thought to find Pittman's grave,

God knows how. It's in Florida maybe, or Alabama, lost among the Stuckey's and Popeye's, the Best Western's and interstates, the Chick-Fil-A's and driving ranges. In all these reveries I never know what to say, and haven't thought to speak in one of them. I simply take a knee, shut my eyes, and put a hand to stone. Touch is everything.

My MOTHER OBVIOUSLY HAD HANDS TOO, tiny ones, something I never realized before proposing to Karen, and wouldn't have had my sisters not mentioned it. My mom bequeathed me her wedding ring, which she received when my dad's mother passed months before I was born. At twenty-six I assumed I'd need it soon, but in the shock of bereavement vouchsafed it to a sister. Way, though, led to way, fling to fling, and with Connecticut leading to Vermont leading to California leading to Alaska—with twenty-six turning to forty throughout—the ring was forgotten. Back in Queens, however, needing it quickly, I hustled to Connecticut, where my oldest sister set me straight.

"You're a guy," she said, "so you wouldn't think to mention this, but trust me, mention it. Mom had little hands with abnormally slender fingers, so the ring part is narrow. Really narrow. Stress that. Otherwise she'll be embarrassed."

When I called my other sister in Colorado, she corroborated in her less-delicate style.

"Jesus," she said. "If you start out with her thinking she has fat fingers, you're sunk."

Funny I never noticed that, about her hands, given all that a mother's hands do. They change you, bathe you, feed you, teach you to stack, teach you to write, teach you to read, teach you tie your shoes. They take temperatures, provide medicine, apply pressure to bloodied knees. They grip your own hands when you shake with fever, hold you tight when necessary, and, if needed, whack you. Through all that I should have seen it, but didn't, likely because two of those fingers once felt like the thunderbolts of Zeus, and still do.

It's not that my mother couldn't small talk. She could, and well, but preferred to dive deep. I can't remember how old I was when she told me that both she and my father were virgins when they married, but I certainly didn't know what *virgin* meant. When *One Flew Over the Cuckoo's Nest* came out, I was seven. We were at the lake cabin alone. It's possible she looked for a sitter, but I doubt it, and if I didn't know what a virgin was, I in no way knew what I'd just seen when we left that theater. After a day, though, hashing it silly, I could have written a passable paper on everything from misandry to misogyny to despotism to the felonious treatment of the deranged to political subversion to whatever the hell McMurphy was doing with that brown-haired lady in the boat cabin.

"Juicy Fruit," my mom finally said. "The whole movie coils into that one line, and you can nearly say the same about being human."

A couple of years earlier, driving beneath the scarlet, bronze, and salmon flesh pigments marking Connecticut's October oak, maple, and hickory mix, I asked her about church.

"Why?" she said, one hand on the wheel, the other dragging a Winston.

"John and Scott are going there on Sunday. They always do. That's why they can never play."

My mom flicked an ash in the tray and angled a purple plume out the window.

"Church is where some people talk to God."

"What's God?"

"No one's sure. It's like love. You can't see it, you sure can't define it, but you know it's there. At least most people do."

"Why do you have to go to church?"

"Well, that's the trick. You don't."

"Where is God?"

A final plume billowed away, then she smooshed the butt before moving her hand through space to thunk my heart twice with a pair of slender fingers.

"Right there," she said. "You'll either find Him or you won't."

My mom didn't hate much, but she hated snakes, convinced that one lurked in the bushes at any moment, poised to take her down whole. If she hated snakes, though, she loved horses in equal share, and by 1980 my pop had made enough from his start-up marketing outfit to consummate one of her dreams, moving us a half mile to a property big enough to build a barn.

"If there's something I hate more than a horse," my dad

said, "I'm not sure what it is. Thank God for them I love your mother."

A couple of years later, with the barn built and both paddock and pastures beveled into the rocky pitch, my mom came to the house one Sunday, interrupting football.

"There's a snake in the paddock," she said.

My dad, eating crackers, brushed a few crumbs off the bench.

"I'll have a look."

"Well you'll have to do more than that. It's huge, and one of the horses is in there."

"It'll be fine," he said, opening the door, walking out into a snake-happy Indian summer. "It'll just slither into the bushes. It's only sunning."

"It'll come back," my mom said, close behind.

I watched a couple of more plays, then boxed up my pop's crackers and put them in a cupboard. This, I thought, ought to be good, and walked outside.

It was good, though not in the manner I'd expected. By the time I slipped around the barn to view the paddock, my dad held a garden rake overhead. The snake was huge. My mom had that right. Though no horse eaters, rat snakes go to six feet and pair a menacing look with a foul temperament. Still, had my dad insisted, it simply would have slithered along the clay and into the woods, never to be seen again. Here, though, the creature raised its head, sliding inches forward, then a few more. The rake came down, narrow end first, and the low-bass crunch mid-body said it all, with the long form now writhing like wind-whirled laces around its new hinge. Having neutralized it, my dad took better aim. Thwack, and that was it. Twenty yards away the horse looked on, consuming straw as it otherwise would have.

A hose went on inside the barn, which meant that my mom was scrubbing down another animal, but my eyes stayed on my pop. He loves snakes. Not in the oddball python-around-the-neck fashion, but in stark admiration. The legless mobility, the dislocating jaw, the seeing-eye tongue, their subtle station in the greater gestalt, all the sinister properties we've ascribed to them. Everything. This one he toed a time or two, then bent to grasp it behind the eyes before walking toward the woods, the tail tickling the paddock. Ducking the fence, he pulled the limp corpse through, then laid the long body beneath an oak. Shakespeare couldn't define love in the way my mom once meant, and I certainly can't, but I do know what it looks like.

Twelve years later my mom died in the common way, cancer-shot and hospitalized. Lymphoma killed her, two years in the brewing, and when it turned it turned quickly, leaving us nineteen days of oncology-ward vigils before she went her way and we stayed put.

Two days from her time she slipped into a coma, simply breathing out of habit through the end. This gave us seventeen farewell days, number fifteen of which was the last time I saw her walk. I'd taken the invisible fencing job a couple of months before and drove to the hospital each evening straight from the mud-and-briar filth of long, wire-burying days, every yard of which was a welcome purgative. On one such night I rode the elevator to the sixth floor, walking into the hall to see my mom's be-gowned body laboring in the opposite direction, with my father pacing the IV stand alongside while the other hand braced her lumbar. A window at hall's end looked over a gravel rooftop wedged between our floor and the brick wall of a higher wing. Two chairs had been placed there, face out, and as I signed in at the front desk my dad helped my mother into one then sat in the other.

Her hair had grayed through in two weeks, and even at twenty yards I could see the jaundiced tincture increasingly staining her hands. My pop slid his seat a half foot closer then reached, taking one of those hands and letting ten twined fingers, thirty-nine years, three kids, and all the hells and heavens of a successful marriage hang between them. I didn't approach. A few gulls cupped the manufactured thermals rising out of the industrial coolant system on the roof outside, and in the dying day a row of pigeons lined the ledge of the facing wing, their daily droppings ossifying on the bricks beneath.

A few years before, I'd worked at a gas station, often listening to the owner, a booze-puffed Finn who at thirteen had driven staff cars in the Russo-Finnish War. When needed, he'd shouldered a rifle.

"Trust me," he once said. "Nobody dies well."

I don't know if that's true, but in every death we re-learn how pathos-riddled our little lives really are. Taking a seat near the front desk, I looked down the hall. With gulls hovering beyond the glass and the pigeons idling, I watched my parents live out one final portion between them.

Over the next year something new arose. My pop wasn't well. Likely fostered by his addled upbringing, he heretofore cloistered all pain, and in twenty-six years I'd never seen him down.

"Don't let that fool you," my mom once said. "Everybody gets down. He's learned to bury it."

Her death changed that. Afterward, he lived alone for a year in the house where he'd raised us before common sense saw my oldest sister move in with her own growing family, freeing him to relocate to smaller, less spook-tinged quarters.

During that initial year, though, I lived one town over, often stopping by after work. Most nights found him in a chair, eating cheese, half-following a baseball game. By November it had turned to basketball, but we at least had weekends to drive up to Pennsylvania, hunting old familiar orchards in old familiar ways, and that Thanksgiving brought one of our best trapping seasons.

"Seven mink in seven days," he said, hanging the last trap in the shed. "That's directed from the other side."

Still, as winter settled in, he looked like a soon-to-fall boxer. The hands stayed up, the body weaved, but the legs were gone. By spring, too, I'd moved to Vermont, deepening the worry.

ALOFT

"I look; you look; he looks; we look; ye look; they look."

—PIP, IN MOBY DICK

OVER THE SUMMER I talked to my dad frequently, but the calls were brief, and revealing only for that brevity. By September, though, two fissures had appeared, boding a thaw. First, he'd met someone, and a good someone.

"Your dad isn't afraid of much," my mom said days before dying, "but he's terrified of being alone. Most men are. He'll re-marry not long after I die. Don't be a jerk about it."

Honor thy mother and honor thy father, we're told, so being a jerk wasn't an option, but he'd found a proper fit, making this particular obligation perfunctory.

Second, we'd discovered Vermont, specifically its grouse and woodcock populations. Route 100, right up the Mad River Valley. If America has a prettier stretch I haven't seen it, with every square foot a New England postcard—worn, stubbornly-statured mountains bathed in trees, remnant pastures kept by equally stubborn farmers, and here-and-there towns comprised of the same post office-general store-clapboard church trinity.

My company had stationed me mid-state, charging me with invisibly fencing Vermont's and New Hampshire's southern halves, and I spent the summer cross-hatching the region six days a week. By September, when upland game hunting started, I had more feral orchards and new-growth aspen marked than could be hunted in a season, much of it strewn along the Mad River, and having hunted the first two Sundays alone, I called my pop.

"You have to see this," I said.

Though burnished with the past year-and-a-half's plaintive torpor, a bit of the old buoyancy had re-surfaced.

"I'll be there," he said.

Landscape can be known from a thousand angles. If my dad had to dig a foundation, log forty acres, plant forty more for corn, twenty others for peaches, or do much of anything else he'd simply stand there, befuddled. Put him in grouse country, though, in any season, and he's fluent. While I'd hunted Vermont a couple of times, I'd lacked the proper interpreter, but not now. Five yards into the first cover—pockets of apple and birch pinched by hemlock, all terraced down to a modest, hardwood-dominated creek—my dad spoke before we split to our accustomed thirty yards.

"This won't be like the lake. There are more active farms there, open country, isolating the covers. Grouse bunch in to where they won't fly over fields until there's no option. That's why we get so many flushes. This is deep, unbroken woods, not much to hold them. We'll have to work harder here."

We did work harder, that weekend and the next, then all fall. He came up every Friday night, hunting alone on Saturday. After a night of college football, we spent Sunday hunting together. The covers became familiar, and memories piled up.

It had been a warm fall, unseasonably so, but still, by early November, with the last foliage down, we didn't expect to see another woodcock. Structured more like shorebirds than those of upland forests, woodcock use their long, needle bill to route bottomlands for earthworms, their exclusive diet. They need thawed ground, then, and migrate as far south as necessary, usually wintering along the lower Mississippi. Most years, all are gone from New England before Halloween. If the ground stays soft, however, and the worms active, you'll find the odd straggler.

One of our favorite covers was an extension of that first. Turning off Route 100, we drove two miles up a dirt road and parked, pushing the terraced apple and birch down to the mountain creek, which we straddled nearly to the road through poor habitat, mostly open hardwood. A hundred yards from the highway, though, the mountain leveled a bit before the creek joined the Mad, and within that flat a two-hundred yard aspen strip had grown level with an old orchard, a leave-behind from the days when every farm ministered a cider crop.

In such stretches one or two flushes is a disappointment. Here, too, woodcock in particular had been thick, and earlier on I'd shot one near the dirt road, where we ended each hunt, while my pop had downed two others on successive days. Now, however, with recent frosts and a memory bank insisting that all woodcock are gone by the turn of the month, grouse alone were anticipated, startling us all the more when, as we entered the first aspens, a long-billed bird nearly hopped off my boot.

Though overlapping in habitat, grouse and woodcock are wildly different. Spectacular flyers, grouse are equally mobile afoot and often get themselves out of trouble without a hunter ever knowing they were there. Woodcock do this too, though by alternate means. Not great flyers, they're even worse walkers, scarcely able to take three consecutive strides. With mottled, pale brown plumage, though, they look like any patch of detritus, from hardwood sheds to white pine. They know this, and frequently sit tight until you're a pace off, popping aloft like slung skeet before winging away. On the fly they're slower than grouse, skewing timing. Such was the case here, and after I'd missed my two shots my dad missed his.

"Well," he said, breaking his gun, replacing two spent shells with two live, "at least there weren't any witnesses."

He shut the gun, then parted the undergrowth in coming my way.

"O.K." he said. "It's thick in here, so I lost the sightline, but my guess is he didn't cross that springlet. The watercress makes just enough of an opening there and he probably sat down to avoid it. Let's get a little further upslope, then angle down to where the dirt road meets the highway. If he flies up the mountain we've lost him, but if we get him going toward the road we'll get at least one more flush. Pay attention around that spring."

Gliding through the dense aspen shoots and down-spiraled apple bowers, he stationed himself on the uphill post. I waited, then on his signal paralleled him toward the as yet unseen watercress.

The farm had likely been abandoned around 1900, making this cover as fleeting as the rest, with the preferred second growth now losing favor to forest succession. Mingled in the cover's periphery, yellow birch and rock maple already crowned the aspens, strangling the apples every year with increasing shade. Still, another hunting generation would find birds here.

Stopping is critical to hunting woodcock, as their camouflage makes their chief hope not to fly, but to let any threat simply wander through. Crouching beneath an apple's dangled spread, I straightened, then stopped, noting the spring's spare clearing ten yards off through heavy brush. Porcupines had stripped bark from several apple branches here and an even-tempoed tap above had me raise my eyes to the expected sight, a hairy woodpecker trying to vibrate insects from bark. Barred black and white, a scarlet patch painted on the back of its head, it twice rounded an upper branch before flying. I followed it to the next tree, then turned, running toward the single shotgun blast and my dad's rapidly fading form.

One shot meat, two shots maybe goes the expression, and in conjunction with the lone bang my pop's reaction meant a hit. The growth was a struggle, my boots sinking in the spring's black mud, but when a bird goes down progress must be made.

By the time I caught up to my panting father, he'd already laid down his hat and gun, sixty yards from the shot.

"He got up way ahead," he said, eyes roving deciduous litter. "I didn't expect that, and certainly didn't expect to hit it. He sailed on us, too, but this mark should be close."

Woodcock are among the toughest birds to find without dogs, but to date my dad and I hadn't lost one, nor a grouse.

"Dying birds often use the last thing left to them," he'd told me long ago. "They spread their wings and lie flat, using those leaf-patterned feathers to stay hidden. I've looked for an hour a couple of times before finding them, usually right near the mark. It's common to miss them on the first go through."

The mark is where you start. Hunters lay their gun down where they think the bird fell, then search in outward expanding circles. If no bird is found in a twenty yard circumference, the rings are re-traced toward the center. It's a hands-and-knees affair, with every crevice snouted and every weed bent aside. We commenced, and ten seconds later it was over.

"Jesus," my dad said, rising to both knees. "Look at this."

It was four yards from his hat. Wings spread, head down, stone dead.

"We damned near stood on him."

Pushing off the ground, he rose.

Words detect so little, so little of import. In that motion to erect himself I noticed what I hadn't in previous conversations: that he'd shuffled off the bulk of his grief, doffing it somewhere unknown, like snakeskin. In the profound losses it never leaves—how could it?—but at some point without anyone's awareness, the aggrieved's most of all, sorrow's most suffocating portions simply fall away, dissipating the pall attending them. The first time I shot a grouse my father shook my hand, but in fifteen subsequent years we hadn't thought to do so since. Upon picking up the woodcock, though, my empty hand reached for his.

"Congratulations," I said.

He grasped, then nodded.

Christ knows how many hands shape even a single life, but in that petering out orchard, squeezing my pop's palm, I felt at least the stains of purple smoke and snapper blood, and in that one vein it may be that we really do never die.

I HAVE NO IDEA if my mom's passing freed my father and me to wander, but it might have. She'd been quite rooted to her Connecticut farm, making it unlikely that she and my dad would have relocated. For my part, I'll never know if her genial gravity would have kept me close in spite of her own hobbled wanderlust, but either way, when she passed it did seem that my father and I lost our respective orbits and, though it didn't happen immediately, he ended up in Scottsdale, Arizona, not long after re-marrying,, while I, by way of Vermont and a brief California spell, wound up in Yakutat, Alaska.

Retrospect is of little use. Even if hindsight is 20/20, it doesn't always clarify. We often eulogize the deceased as set free, but it could be that the bereaved as often experience emancipation, untethered to live a different life than they otherwise might have, however much they regret that exchange. In both my father's case and my own, neither of us will ever know.

Regardless, not long after I handed my dad that woodcock, the Philadelphia-based Invisible Fence, Inc. put word out that things across California were awry, and that they were recruiting permanent help to rectify that. Though I'd quickly come to love Vermont, "Wagons Ho" was all I could say. Several states hold mythical stations in the American mind—Kentucky, Louisiana, Montana among them—but California may top the list. It's the last stop westward, with all the fulfillment and heartbreak that has always meant. After an interview I took the job, moving a couple of months later.

Things were certainly awry. Customer service had been nearly non-existent and many dealers had folded up without a word. In the ensuing chaos, management didn't know where to put the Eastern transplants, and after starting in San Diego, I spent a couple of months in Los Angeles followed by two more in Santa Barbara before somewhat settling in San Francisco's village-like Sunset District, the lone employee for all of California's vast center. I enjoyed it there, but it didn't seem much different than what I'd left. A typical day would find me first in Marin County, then Berkeley, then the peninsula, then on down to Palo Alto. If I saw the gamut while there, though, the region-wide strip mall/cul-de-sac scapes might have been Connecticut. A year passed, and once the customer base stabilized, the job seemed to have run its course. Fortunately, I received a timely phone call.

Two years before I'd spent a few days in Yakutat, an isolated town half way between Juneau and Anchorage. A friend who worked in the Forest Service had drawn me there for a visit, but he'd been summoned to a forest fire in the Rockies. I used his car to do a little salmon fishing and see the considerable sights. A few days, though, isn't much, and while deeply impressed, I never thought to return, but as these things go I'd also met a woman there, Indiana-derived and terrific. We'd kept in touch. She even visited once in Vermont, then again in San Francisco, and by the time I'd started poking around for another job she called. The Alaska fish and game department had offered her a two-month slot working a fish weir, one that required a partner. The work was easy, counting salmon through what amounts to a picket fence, but involved two people living together in an isolated cabin, making friendly relations vital.

"The boss said he doesn't care who I pick as long as we get along," she said. "What do you think?"

I didn't think long. Despite having already seen Yakutat, I'd never shaken my childhood fantasies of living deep in wilderness—running trap lines, hunting, just wandering around out there, alone. Two months wasn't long, but at least I could pile up some money while looking for more permanent work. As often happens to so many people, though, I went somewhere for a summer and stayed.

I wasn't settled enough—or mature enough, if there's a difference—for a permanent relationship, so while things didn't work out with my weir partner, the two-month stint ended with additional opportunities, and in short order I was able to garner over eight months of work a year piecing various projects together across Southeast Alaska, the kite tail streaming off Anchorage along the Canadian coast. For the remaining months, the fish and game department needed someone to maintain the bunkhouse they'd erected, and as few cared for the long winters, the spot was mine to refuse, which I decidedly didn't.

Spring work meant smolt camps, usually staged on fly-in-only rivers with a crew of four sent in for two months. When juvenile salmon are ready to migrate seaward, they brighten and grow in preparation, then flood downriver. They can be trapped in large numbers then, and we placed a coded-wire tag in their snout upon doing so, recovering the tags when they returned as adults, allowing biologists to infer various data.

Once smolt season was through, I spent summer and fall in Yakutat, which has some fame for the Situk River, more of a stream that, for its size, boasts, large runs of chinook, sockeye, coho, and pink salmon, with the first three having great commercial value. Relative to most fish, salmon are somewhat easy to manage as they can be accurately counted in rivers, my primary job. Some were counted by air from single engine planes, some by boat, while smaller creeks were indexed by foot. Counting wasn't the whole of it, but everything else— tagging fish, netting fish, measuring fish, taking scales off fish, even killing fish—revolved around that aim.

Much of the work I did alone, normally a departmental taboo. The guy who hired me, though, retired before the first year was out. His replacement, Gordie, had performed my job for thirty years before they promoted him elsewhere. When the Yakutat management slot opened, he took it, and quickly became much more friend than boss. He'd come up in the job prior to any liability concerns and didn't think anything of someone spending a day or more out in the woods alone.

"Just make noise," he said. "The bears won't bug you."

A convivial guy, Gordie was a fountainhead of good stories and jolly wit. "You can hang your brain on a hook and tag smolt," he said before I flew off to my first camp. He lived in a small cabin, an entire wall of which contained his jazz collection, and Friday nights throughout summer and fall a few of us gathered habitually for music and drinks, but mostly for good company.

Yakutat itself sits atop the Tongass National Forest, a West Virginia-sized tract running down through Juneau. Ice once covered it all. When it receded, the Eyak people found what is now Yakutat. They were assimilated soon after by the Tlingit, a conglomerate of clans who based a Viking-ish culture out of the place, setting off in deep canoes to barter with and pillage other tribes. Two hundred and fifty years ago a few Spaniards sailed in, explorers, then left, and not long after that, in 1795, the Russians came, fur-traders. They wore out the sea otters and seals and eventually the Tlingit's, who threw them out, and sometime later the Americans showed up. After decades of stark oppression, the two peoples have sufficiently co-mingled sexually and culturally to have cooled to a marbled magma—swirls of resentment and détente, mutual scorn and admiration—and now 700 such residents live alongside Monti Bay, an Alaskan Gulf incursion. The rest of it, the

Yakutat Forelands—two hundred miles up the coast one way, two hundred miles down the other—belongs to the fish and the animals and every citizen of the United States. Beyond the airport, a few inland clear-cuts, several fishing lodges, the ramshackle gillnetters' camps along the estuaries, and the thirty-mile Harlequin Lake road, there's nothing but rainforest on the flats, ice in the mountains, and salmon streams. If you're a land-developer it's an abomination. If you're a Puritan it's the Devil's last retreat. If you're anything else it may not be heaven, but it's very close.

In time, I'd come to know all this, but upon first realizing that I'd be there longer than expected, I was anxious to get out on the land itself, something I did in earnest early that first spring. Still unbeknownst to me, this coincided with a growing cosmological unrest that would dominate the coming decade.

If you're new to it, April in Alaska can surprise. Like other places, it's a month of great awakening. Every nook of the natural world seems to have a phenomenon or two that only people familiar with the land know about, and Yakutat is no different. If buds are still locked in their branches and snows still common, a great many other signs marking winter's dissolution appear. Light, for one, finally overtakes the dark. In the rain forests of south-east Alaska the dismal seven hours of weak sunlight are a memory by April, and with the increasing light the winter wrens perk up, scolding high in the dripping spruce boughs for the first time in months. The season's first thrushes and warblers arrive as well. Ducks, too, are back, rafting up in the estuaries by the thousands, feeding and resting before completing the last leg north. And the hooligan come in, a soft, smelt-like fish that pours into the rivers in numberless formations, a crucial event. Animals all winter scrape by on the austerity of the land and the scraps of wolf-kills, when suddenly endless lines of easily-caught, oil-laden fish return to the waterways.

A few years before, I didn't know much about hooligan, or anything else in the area for that matter. Now, though, early April, I paddled out of Yakutat, initially on an extended estuary, then fifteen miles or so up a river into the foothills of a considerable mountain chain. I didn't know how far I'd get, but gave myself the full week.

The Yakutat Forelands are a vast wilderness with very few miles of roads. Boats allow access to otherwise inaccessible territory, and I was eager to become far more familiar with a fascinating place that looked like it might be home, at least for a while.

I'd bought a canoe the previous fall. The air was crisp but the paddling warm, and while the clouds spit occasional rain, overall things the first day were pleasant. The initial leg was simple, a five-mile creek downstream to the estuary. About half way down I ran into the first hooligan, moving in great hordes, slow but steady, pressing upstream to spawn. Eagles were everywhere, dotted in the towering spruce. Restored by the hooligan after a winter of semi-dormancy, the big birds cackled and soared, picking occasional fights with each other. Kingfishers, too, chatted and darted among the lower alders, while ravens—intelligent, weird in the old way—communicated their strange language from the trees and the air.

As I steered the canoe along the stream's lazy turns, my eyes rested mostly on the metallic fish. As individuals they struggled mightily. As a group they were unstoppable. Scores of corpses, stiff and drained of color, gathered in the sandy, gentle eddies along the bottom. Others, near death, swirled here and there in dazed circles. In the main, though, the juggernaut was unfazed. Over on the bank, yards away, I heard a great huff, then what I thought was a familiar sound. I looked up. Having forgotten where I was, I expected to see a horse cantering away. It wasn't. A brown bear, lithe and worn from hibernation, sped across the open bank toward the brush. I'd seen them before, but never so close and never so well. Running the right way, in the opposite direction from me, for a few strides every muscle was visible, throbbing and huge beneath thick flesh and thicker fur. I understood then why they tell you not to run. It wasn't the first time I'd felt humbled and puny in the woods, but it was the first time I felt utter vulnerability before a single creature. Like the birds, it too had come down for the hooligan.

When I got to the estuary the tide had just turned, carrying me along the wide water paralleling the shore. A spare, dark sandy spit blocked the ocean, but the acoustics of the gentle breakers outside crept over the bar. By now I was miles from town. I'd been alone in the woods countless times, but this was different. Behind me, westward, lay the village, three hours by canoe, while yards to the south rolled the Pacific. To the north and east were river and forest, flat beneath the mountains, peopleless for a hundred and fifty miles or more.

Even when helped by the tide, paddling a canoe takes time. Stroke after stroke you plod along, marking progress. Beyond a long island that split the river, a smaller creek joined the estuary. About here the tide stopped and I started pushing against current. This area is known as the Flats, a long series of ever-changing sandbars and shifting channels. The land and water track on such a plane as to make mirages common, where what is sand and what is water are indistinguishable even at close distances.

Without the occlusion of the tide, the hooligan were noticeable again, and in far greater numbers than before. Every stroke of the paddle knocked a couple of dozen out of formation, opening a space until they recovered. Birds were here, too, ducks at first. Pintails, scaup, teal, and mallards—all gathered in mixed flocks. They never let me close, having from Alaska to Mexico and back to Alaska learned that my kind hunts their kind with startling vigor.

It was around here that I heard, then saw, the first seal. A deep-throated splash sounded behind me. I turned and looked, seeing nothing but a widening swirl. A few strokes later and they were all around, a couple of dozen or more. The hooligan are a great boon to them, too. They follow the multitudes into the river mouths then up toward the shallows, by turns gorging themselves and hauling out in great pods upon the sandbars. I'd paddled into a frenzy. Several came close to the boat, their enormous, curious black eyes regarding whatever they saw in me with the same intellect I'd sensed in that dying grouse's eye on Jacob's Ladder nearly two decades before. As each seal surfaced it let out a loud breath, like a pipe bursting under pressure. They did this repeatedly, bobbing in a staggered circle around the boat, composing an odd staccato. After a while they lost interest, and soon the last of them was behind me.

There's a vitality to mirage light. The horizon seems blurred, jittering slightly in varied textures. For a moment, a quarter-mile past the seals, I thought the flats were covered in snow. Acres were blanched in quivering whites. I hadn't, though, noticed the sound. Seagulls, thousands of them, stood on the sandy banks or floated together in the coursing water, squealing away, each taking what must have been its first easy meal in months. I was a few hundred yards from the main body. A ragged line—much closer—led up to it. The first bird took off, then another, then many more in succession. Soon the whole group spooked, several thousand birds lifting at once, making a great fuss. After the initial confusion, though, a decisive direction emerged, and they headed directly at me. For a moment the explosion of such energy after miles of quietude left me motionless. As they drew nearer, however, I realized what was going to happen. My raincoat was draped over the canoe's yoke, and I rushed to put it on as the first gulls flew over. I pulled the hood over my head, knelt on the bottom, and tucked my bare hands into my body. Like a summer squall, the first drops hit sporadically, thick and hard, followed by the deluge. All I could do was hunch down. For thirty seconds the droppings hit my back and the boat indiscriminately, and the absurdity of it, indignity even, caught me and I broke out laughing, still curled into myself. When the popping on the water stopped I looked up. The birds were over the beach by then.

Laughing is peculiar, a highly social phenomenon. We don't do it much when we're alone, and when we do, it accentuates our solitude. No one was there to see it, and I realized the laugh wouldn't be complete until I returned home and recounted it. Still, I didn't mind. That day wasn't far off. I beached the boat and gave everything a thorough scrub-down—my gear, my jacket, the boat—then paddled the remainder of the estuary, eventually turning north toward the mountains lying somewhere miles ahead through shifting fogs.

I camped twice on the way up. In a canoe you can make about a mile an hour upstream. With twelve hours of daylight, that gave me nine hours of comfortable traveling time. The first night, with daylight just starting to fade, I pitched the tent on a high bank covered in willow and alder in a crescent-shaped clearing not much bigger than the tent itself. Next I gathered wood. Fires aren't always possible in a rainforest, but it hadn't come down hard lately and if you look for dead branches on the still-living trees enough dry wood can usually be found. I'd brought plenty of food but with the hooligan there for the taking I decided to conserve. Wading in, I easily plucked a dozen small fish from the cold river. On the opposite bank, a mink loped beneath the dangling brush, slipping into the current and coming out with a fish of its own. Otter tracks covered the sandbars around me, their scaly scat left among the clumsy foot-prints. On one bar a larger set of prints—a brown bear's—blotted out those of the otters.

Hooligan smoke well but other than that are quite bland, even mealy. Still, you never seem to eat much when camping and if nothing else the oil was welcome. I hung the other food and some gear in one of the few spruce along the lower river, pulled the canoe onto the bank, then cracked a book by the dying fire. All day in a canoe wears you down, though, and I didn't last long. When I rose from beside the fire, a beaver startled in the river below, slapping its tail against the water before diving down. I wondered if anything else out there heeded the warning. I went to the tent, put a loaded shotgun by my side, then slipped inside the sleeping bag. Outside I heard nothing. Though birds were starting to migrate through, they wouldn't sing at night, and it was too early in the year for insects, which in Southeast are nothing like what interior Alaska experiences. It's rare nowadays to fall asleep in total darkness and total silence, and quite pleasant. I woke many hours later, still in silence, with the first, steely glow of day fingering the tent fabric.

That day was a travel day. I figured if I had a shot at getting near the mountains I needed a lot of miles before nightfall, and the canoe was loaded before full light. I hadn't had much experience paddling up a river, but the logic is simple. Running water is mostly a continuum of pools and riffles. Riffles are usually shallow and better to walk through, while most pools have an eddy of some sort, either reversing or neutralizing the current. It doesn't take long to find the easiest routes, and after a while the rhythm of walking and paddling, paddling and walking, becomes ruminative, with abstract thought partitioning the conscious mind from physical labor, making the latter nearly involuntary. I scared a moose around one bend, who'd been crossing the stream on a shallow gravel bar. It panicked, wheeling around and angling upstream to the other bank, a foolish move. The water deepened here and in a few strides he was in over his head, swimming. I stopped mid-river, alternating the paddle from side to side to keep the boat steady. The moose had picked a place too steep to climb, and after a few frantic attempts slipped clumsily into the current, where it regained traction in the gravel. Standing, it assessed me for a minute or more before recovering its composure. I was in deep water myself and didn't worry. It began moving in the unrhythmic, lumbering strides of its breed, then crossed on the original route, ascending the bank in a crash of brush and motion. When we're outside of nature we think of it fondly as a place where everything aligns in harmony. It isn't. Animals—like us—err all the time. I paddled forward and got out to walk over the bar where the creature had crossed. Absent any fanfare, the river I now moved through would swallow either me or that moose if either of us let it, and without any thought that we're aware of.

Clouds had thickened over the day and instead of rain a thick, oatmealish snow fell. It clung to everything in the boat and as it melted filled the bottom with slush and water, spoiling the ballast. Every half-mile or so I pulled ashore, emptying the gear and turning over the canoe. That night I camped in a thick spruce grove, where the heavy trees trapped enough heat to leave the ground wet but clear. I didn't attempt a fire, spending most of the dwindling daylight stringing tarps and stowing gear in order to keep everything dry. Sleep came easily, and I again woke at first light.

By dawn, five inches of new snow had covered the gravel bars and open banks, adding to the old patches that in places remained three feet deep, all reminders that while spring makes headway here in April, winter still has a vote. After loading the canoe I took a moment and looked in the pool at my feet, noticing something I hadn't the previous day. The hooligan were gone. Sometime the day before, lost in the prolonged reveries common to solitude and physical exertion, I'd paddled above their range. Looking up, I found something else, too. I'd gone much farther than I'd thought. The clouds had broken slightly during the night, and between strips of fog I saw mountains, larger and much closer than I expected. By midday I'd made it, not to the mountains themselves—mostly barren and packed in year-round snow—but to the foothills which, if not large, are lush with timber and other life.

Like all rivers, this one changes character closer to its source. The grade is steeper and the water shallower. The land in southeast Alaska is also rapidly expanding, as the glacial till of its many rivers spills out into the ocean ton after ton, adding to the beaches. The further inland you go, then, the older the land, a fact reflected in the vegetation. Here, upriver, spruce dominate the banks, marking the ground's older age.

This far up choices were necessary. Smaller streams and branches make large rivers what they are, and several similar-sized creeks conjoined at varying spots, forcing decisions.

There are maps of this area, and good ones, but not so detailed as to delineate every tributary. As I picked my way I wondered how many people across how many years had made these same choices. Starting a century ago, natives probably made them all the time. More recently it receives less traffic. Cartographers and biologists have made forays in here, but none in earnest for a couple of decades. Every couple of years or so, too, a bear hunter heads this way on a day trip. Other than that, it's clean. I picked what I thought were the straightest routes to the closest hills, realizing now that no one really knew where I was nor cared what decisions I made.

The last stream was little more than a hop-across affair, opening up from spruce forest to an enormous, willow-laden muskeg abutting the foothills. It looked like beaver country and it was. Dams new and old clogged the creek, along with the many rivulets feeding it. Beavers are the great providers wherever they go. The ponds attract every resident creature, who come to feed either on the thick vegetation that itself feeds on the swampy ground, or upon other creatures. Pulling the canoe over one dam—a jumble of whittled willow limbs and mortared mud—a great canine print remained in a faded patch of snow. A wolf had been here. Salmon, too, who supply the bulk of nutrition to both plants and animals in this country, are greatly aided by beavers. Juveniles thrive in the ponds, with the deep, dark water offering fine refuge from predators, while the nutrient-rich waters provide better than usual fodder. Spring time is smolting time, and clouds of thumb-long fish—their bodies rapidly changing—darted to cover from time to time as I passed over them. Mergansers, too—both common and hooded—spooked at my approach. They were here for the gathering fish, and as spring went on and the smolt began their migration, the birds would follow.

The mountains, though still miles away, lorded over me with bright sunlight and gleaming snow-pack. Nearer, only a few hundred yards away, the first spruce-covered hillocks lay. I paddled until the stream grew too narrow for the boat, then got out to find a camping spot.

After pulling the boat on the bank, I headed for the first hummock. The sun beat down on the muskeg, and I could see plenty of dry wood in the standing willow. I kept moving. As the ground gradually rose, the willow gave way to blueberry, then the first spruce. At the base of the little hill, nestled between two large evergreens, draped in lichen, a deep spring bubbled from the ground, the pumping water gently roiling the pool's dark surface. It spilled over the back to form a substantial springlet that ran by my feet. I headed up the incline, passing through the spiny devil's club and over several windfalls. The top wasn't more than a hundred-yard climb.

The peak was actually three peaks, several soft summits split by gentle depressions. One of these was flat and soft and I cleared a little vegetation before returning to the boat for the gear. Humping it back, I strung tarps and pitched the tent, then made several trips up and down to the muskeg, carrying as much dead willow as I could each time. The high-pressure system that had brought the sun had also dropped the temperature. A couple of hours' daylight remained after camp was set, and I walked the narrow stream I'd paddled up, where a bear trail made the bushwhacking tolerable.

Remains of the previous autumn's salmon were everywhere, strewn about like eroded fossils. The bears come at that time, having followed the fish to their spawning grounds, where salmon are simple to catch in the shallow, oxygen-rich riffles they need to lay eggs. Bears often only eat the brains, leaving the rest for the jays, mink, ravens, and other opportunists. At the end only scattered bones remain, every year leaching their sea-borne particles to the young, burgeoning forest. Life, though, was certainly more than remnant here. In the dark, tannic waters fry and smolt moved beneath the overhangs at my approach, themselves beneficiaries of the nutrients the dying adults bequeath every season to the young of their kind. The little fish now at my feet would return one day to do the same. Out over the ocean, far away, the sun dropped quickly, merging with the horizon in a deep, uniform orange. I turned, walking the same trail back to camp.

The fire started easily. Wood rarely gets completely dry here but this stuff was close. Through the spruce canopy stars sparkled in every gap. Other than the gentle crackling of the fire, the woods were still, at least to my senses. That, though, didn't mean much. Out there, in blackness, mink chased balls of smolt in the beaver ponds, while both saw-whet and great-horned owls kept their vigils for hares and voles, who themselves worked cautiously through the underbrush. Wolves, too, in packs or alone, hunted the foothills and muskegs, looking for everything from moose to mice. A weak column of smoke made its way skyward in the glow of the fire. I was strange in this place, and whatever scents I threw off were no doubt received by the creatures who lived here.

There was no need to move the next day. The camp was comfortable and there was more territory here than I could cover in a month. Besides, after the long days of paddling a respite sounded nice. I woke early to another clear, crisp morning and, after reviving the fire and having breakfast, walked to the adjacent summit and looked on the other side of the hill, where a long, narrow bog spread out of the bottom before rising immediately into larger mountains. The sun had ascended by now and was warming up the flat ground below me. I put some lunch in a day pack, then picked my way downslope.

The muskeg took some doing. I'd left my waders in camp, happy to be in rubber boots after two days of confinement. This side of the hill, though, had active beaver dams. With the brush and the deeper waters making progress difficult, I had to take a more careful route. Right along the mountains ran a wide, shallow, stony creek, and the signs of last year's salmon were thicker than before, with bones atop bones in places. Crossing on an ankle-deep bar, I found a bear trail on the other bank, curving along the contour of the mountain chain. Bears are known for stepping in the same spots year after year, generation after generation, and in several flat stretches the trail was marked by a dozen or more of these ancestral footfalls.

A mile or so down I picked the gentlest incline I could find and started climbing. These hills weren't terribly large either, and I doubt this one rose a thousand feet. Thick blueberry and devil's club, though, grown amongst the many fallen spruce, slowed the climb. Dense and encompassing, the standing timber fractured the sun in thick shards, which then hit the mossy ground at all angles. On two occasions I could hear a flock of kinglets chirping in the needles high above, but never saw their diminutive shapes. Several boulders, huge and out of place in a land with little bedrock, were strewn sporadically about the slope where the glaciers, on their way back into the mountains, had dumped them centuries before. One of these, erect and narrow, had fissured atop the little mountain and stood at the peak like a rent steeple. When I reached it I could see the mountains, now clear and unobstructed.

We forget how much of the earth is unavailable to us, even dry land. Sea water covers the planet's majority, and even a wealth of what land we have gives little succor, being either too dry, too cold, or too raw to support much life. This could probably be said of many people, too. If my father, for instance, gave open access both to his kids and his wife, his own father was largely desolate land. To date I didn't know which side of that divide I occupied. I'd kept intimacy mostly at bay, occasioning a fear that I might eventually track the wrong way, and it could be that I consciously or not preferred excursions such as this to, in part, delay that revelation, if not forego it altogether.

Before me there was little more than rock and snow, stacked in violent elevation. Compared to the hump where I stood, the mostly nameless mountains behind it were sharp, jagged peaks softened below by glacier-worn valleys. Timber was scarce. A few trees clung to the lower elevations, but were dwarves compared to the ranging specimens I'd just walked through. The land, then, was too new, too austere, too beat-up by ice to support much life. In three different passes I could see glaciers rumpled up in the distance, still to the eye but active all the same. Here, as in most of the world, they're in full retreat. I'd looked at maps before I'd come out. These particular glaciers were probably in Canada. I sat against one of the rocks and rested, while a Steller's Jay, cousin to the Blue, agile and deft, regarded me from several branches, keeping silent as it fluttered along its various perches. The lands that are so useful to us now—the Plains, much of the northwest, the still-productive farmland of the mid-Atlantic—all at one time or another benefited from the shape-shifting power of ice. One day the stingy glacier and rock before me would be fertile as well, but that was thousands of years off.

The jay let out a cat's mew, flicked its wings, then sailed downslope in the direction of the ice. I turned, picked my way back down the hill, rewalked the trail, and then crossed the muskeg back to camp.

I re-watered at the spring, filling two plastic jugs. As the sun died I read a book atop the over-turned canoe, then went up the hill to re-kindle the fire. The stars again peered through the spruce, and once more no creature made itself known. As in each of the nights, sleep came soon and deep.

The next morning I woke early to head downriver. By the time the canoe was loaded, the sun, rising steadily behind the peaks, pushed more and more light over the land. The grass in the muskeg had crystallized overnight, crunching beneath my feet as I worked to prepare the boat. When the vessel was in the creek, facing oceanward, I stopped. The mountains—a blackened outline not long ago—gained color and relief in the increasing light, and soon the sun appeared, a thin ribbon of orange peering out from between two peaks. It's impossible to say what makes such things. I know just enough of tectonics and friction to know how landscapes are formed, but what put it all in motion is beyond me, beyond everyone. The sun, rising steadily above the chain, was up now. All of it—the mountains, the glaciers, the ground beneath me—moves all the time, but if I stood here the rest of my life I'd never notice it. If, I thought, for the next thousand years, one human being after another stood where I stand now, none of us together would notice it. Something, though, does, and it's in this way that nature edifies us. If it doesn't give the answers, it puts us in contact with the questions. I stepped in the canoe, took my seat, and pushed off, taking my time over the next couple of days on the way back to town.

I f I ever thought of my Fish and Game job as work I don't remember it. Most of what I did, I probably would have paid to do, and with the short seasonal positions in spring allowing access to different parts of Southeast, I never felt penned up. As the years passed the land became familiar, and with each season I grew to thirst for certain stream counts with nearly the same ardor that I anticipated heading back to Pennsylvania every November to hunt and trap with my dad.

The money was adequate, and I barely spent any besides. While I certainly didn't live off the land, enough salmon could be put up for the year to limit costs, and with all that country right at the doorstep recreation was gratis. Apart from Gordie, too, I worked among great people, which spilled over into a pleasant social life, mostly dinners and beach gatherings. Still, for me as for many, ballast was needed.

People enjoy solitude for different reasons. I love people too much to have ever become a misanthrope, and while I follow politics and certainly vote, it's more from obligation rather than any bug-eyed zeal for what is rendered unto Caesar. If America's wilds, then, are spattered with those who have developed Mongol antipathies toward either centralized government or Corporate America, such last-stand isolation has always been beyond my ken. What continued to drive my need for separation was the same spur it had always been, subjects that since childhood I feared bored the wits out of everyone else—God, nature, and the countless minglings between them. Duck hunting in Yakutat became a favored platform for that, and though I yearned every year for the week each October when my dad would come up, I spent countless days on hunts by myself, with several standing apart in memory.

Ducks aren't readily had on clear days. Early in the season, September, even into mid-October, when they're pouring out of the north, enough birds move around that you don't have to work hard for them. Once it's down to over-wintering ducks, though—the mallards, buffleheads, and golden-eyes—high-pressure systems and the windless, clear skies they bring mean that, since ducks can readily detect danger on such days and tend to stay put, you have to go out to them.

A canoe's a tough way to go after ducks when it's cold, but probably the best. Ice hadn't capped the flowing water yet, and only skimmed the back eddies and swampland to either side. Hunting by foot, or jump-shooting, is an impossibility then, with every step—no matter how tenderly gauged—cracking the air like glass. Even so, the canoe's hard-plastic shell rippled patches here and there on the way to the lake, and two large mallard flocks spooked several hundred yards upstream at the touch of boat to ice. Peering over the spruce wall to the left, the sun soaked the deep-green heads of the drakes, while the hens' mid-wing blues received most of its focus.

The Southeast Alaskan sun dies by degree all through November, and given the area's persistent rains isn't seen much of the year anyway, but if you catch it—and you will—it nestles a fond impression deep within your memory. Some days it's difficult to know much of the world beyond beauty, and so much of what we deem beautiful we owe to light, forgetting all we know about shadow. Tucked tight to the trees, though, themselves muffling the lapping ocean beyond, I paddled in just such a shade.

As always, I wouldn't bother the buffleheads, the golden-eyes either, both off-tasting mollusk eaters. This was November, when all the early-season excitement lapses along with the urge for piles of plucked meat, rich and maroon beneath dimpled, custard skin. Mallards, though, are an early winter prize, dripping with autumn-glutted fat. One would do just fine, unless luck and enough birds were present, where three or four might be nice, promising an evening with friends after the meat had a two-day hang.

I dug the paddle crosswise to the current, angling toward the trees, where the gentle stream—not much wider than the boat—transitioned back from open swamp to the crooked, tangled willows that banked it, all of them now lathered in frost. In the pool below, a burgundy coho listed above her fresh-churned cobble, the caudal spines frayed and yellowed. Above the narrow eddy on the right, now edged in ice, pustules of bloody slush had frozen into the bank. A lone, worm-addled gill raker lay stiff across a willow root, with a curl of scaly scat centering it all, marking where an otter had torn the coho's mate apart the night before. This late run lasts into January, as important to predators and scavengers on this end as the hooligan are in spring. Something flashed in the trees beyond. Earlier in the year, jumpy, I might have been fooled, but this was no duck. A Steller's Jay landed midway up an alder, slanting its head in my direction. I'd pass, and that gill raker would be his.

My best chance was the outlet. The lake is half marsh, with the shores a reedy, amorphous margin, making it difficult to tell where water ends and woodland begins. Puddle ducks—the teal, widgeon, pintails, and mallards—gorge in these grassy flats throughout the migration, while the divers—bluebills and golden-eyes—tend toward the shallow middle, dipping beneath to strain plant life for snails and freshwater shrimp. Now, though, most of the water would be frozen, and all but the mallards, golden-eyes, and late-coming buffleheads gone, with these remaining few forced to the outlet. A combination of water flow, spring activity, and the motion of unspawned cohos—pooling up here in anticipation of their late-run push—keeps the outlet mouth open for some time. There was little doubt this water had drawn down many of the mallards flushed earlier, joining whatever birds were already there. I picked my shotgun off the floor. The outlet wasn't thirty yards away, and I rested the weapon on the yoke before me. Through the frosty limbs, ripples marred the slat of open water ahead.

When so many birds get up, the confusion is bound to send some your way. Most of the mixed flock heard the canoe knock a bent willow I couldn't avoid on the final bend. Two buffleheads, males, ran their pink legs along the water before lifting low. I didn't see the golden-eyes but heard their whistling wings, while the mallards jumped off the surface, flying the length of the lake. Several birds, though, came toward me. I dropped the paddle to the floor and grabbed the gun, getting it to my shoulder. A mallard streamed twenty yards above, veering skyward. He folded at the shot, then plunked the water ten yards off the bow, dead. Another male flew at the edge of my range, the sunlight grabbing his greenhead. I shot, and he spiraled down, landing fifty yards away among the grass humps and drowned willows to the right of the outlet.

It was a foolish shot. Normally I'm more careful, only shooting at birds I'm certain to recover if wounded. This one I'd be lucky to retrieve.

Time is your chief concern and, as with grouse and woodcock, a good mark is critical. Beavers had drowned these trees a generation ago, and the duck had gone down by the gray-trident remains of one such clump. The canoe wouldn't be of use. Too many grass humps and remnant trees crowded the water. I jumped out where the first bird had landed, plucking the limp body from the surface and tossing it in the boat's bottom. Turning, I lined up with my mark and started forward.

I'd forgotten about the ice. Ten yards in I had to turn a hip with each slow, waist-deep shuffle, crumpling the half-inch ice before rotating the other hip and repeating. I went around several grass humps this way, looking down only to see if the water had grown too deep. Passing into sunlight, I finally neared the willow fork, looking for movement, a feather, a dab of blood, anything. When my eyes cleared a final grass hummock I knew I'd been lucky. The ice was thicker here. The duck's weight had cracked but not broken it, and the bird lay face-up in this webbed depression, lolling its sun-dressed head, slowly dying. Had it broken through it would've taken what was left of its life and dove, wrapping itself in weeds. Hunters never find such birds.

I came within five yards, then three, then one, before hearing other ice breaking thirty yards away, straight toward the duck. My eyes lifted but they didn't have to. That measured pace was unmistakable.

Bears shouldn't surprise you this late but they do. We think of them as hibernators but they're not exactly that, and they den-up individually, with some staying active well past the first frosts. Besides, this creek's late coho run always keeps a few lurking about. I knew better, yet every year found myself naively taken aback by the sight of a brown bear in ice or snow. I also know when to be alarmed and when not to. Most bears aren't a threat. They're either far off or make themselves that way upon seeing you. Some, though, are different, but unfortunately such awareness is as susceptible to a lapse as anything else.

I let him stroll right in, well within the distance where

most people tell you to shoot. The sun grazed over the lakeside spruce, shimmering the bristled, frosted hair along its back and shoulders. A large boar, he had his head to the water, smashing ice with each step, speaking all the language of a bear to avoid, but I never moved. The membrane between the horrible and sublime is a permeable one, and those fluids will mix. Each billowed breath rose over his broad face, fastening to the pelt as the muscles and hide passed through it. Its brawn—now a cognate of God—bulged through, even beneath all that iced-up, honey-blond hair and the sluggish fat combs beneath that. Five yards away it stopped, taut, the nostrils pulling in my scent and huffing it back out in easy tempo, each exhalation adding to the hoary halo above. Something twitched. I'd forgotten. A duck was dying between us.

I finally realized how stunted my own breathing had become. Running never does any good, but if enough distance exists you can slowly back away from such a bear, who will most often honor that submission. The time for that, though, had passed. I had one shell left. Birdshot wouldn't do the bear much harm but it wouldn't do it much good either, and I couldn't waste a warning shot. Besides, it had obviously heard the others. I sank to my haunches, looking down, away, but with a peripheral eye to the duck, whose serrated tongue now poked between the yellow bill halves resting on the ice. A blood splotch stained its belly, and the light had left its pearl-brown eye. Gauging the distance, I looked further away, then reached a hand back, slowly, listening for any nuanced change in the gruff breaths beyond. Flickering my fingers, I tickled the duck's down, pinching a tuft and sliding it my way. I shrank, lower, and lower again, waiting. Ice broke. My finger curled around the trigger, but the splintering shards grew distant, not near, and I craned my head to see the bear ambling out the way it had come.

It takes a while for the blood to come back. I'd lost all sensation below the shoulders and remained squatted until feeling returned. My breath evened, then I waded through the broken ice path I'd made before, sidling the dead duck into the canoe alongside the other. I pushed the boat downstream, taking my seat above the stiffening birds. A kingfisher flushed, undulating its way to a new willow perch. The sun had dipped, touching only the distant mountains now in a nimble array of pink.

Weeks before I'd driven a couple of wildlife biologists to various water systems. They were preparing a bear study and scouting places to catch them. One mentioned that the brown bear's Latin name had been shortened recently for sensitivity purposes, from *Ursos arctos horribilis* to *Ursos arctos*. Paddling away, I thought they might as well keep going. *Mundus formosus, mundus terribilis* is all the taxonomy we really need.

WHEN MY FATHER SPENT a winter in Arizona I didn't think much of it. When he returned and said he'd like to live there I thought he was kidding. When he moved there just months later, the year after I'd settled in Yakutat, I thought he was nuts.

At the time I could barely picture the desert itself, let alone him in it. His feet belonged on dirt—fertile, moist, and rich—not on barren sand. He was accustomed to swift, mossy creeks shaded by oak and maple, and the distinction of four seasons. What would his strides know of broken sandstone, baked in the sun, or of cactused arroyos? His heart moved to the red of a cardinal bundled in an apple branch, bright and rosy against fresh snow. What could lizards and javalenas offer him, a man who each spring thirsted for the warbler return, delineating species beneath the foliage of trout streams? While remarriage had proved a boon, I was comforted by that

147

before visiting. I simply couldn't place him among cacti. To me it wasn't his home, and because of that I assumed his efforts wouldn't purchase, that he'd shake off his foolish notion and soon return east. My first visit, though, taken for a week in March before my Fish and Game work revived, quickly disabused any idea that he wasn't at home in Arizona, and as it usually does, walking provided the necessary tutelage.

No place shrinks us like the desert. While mountains, timber, and prairies have reductive powers, there's nothing like a desert to contract the sense of self. As vast and enigmatic as these others are, they possess water, sometimes in great quantities, others in lesser amounts, but either way the substance we need most is there. Whether it's a broad river, a deep lake, or the spidery rivulets thatching hillsides, our own bodies mimic a watershed's vascular nature, and we take note of the thick, verdant vegetation that it sustains. If we can't hear a flowing stream or see a still pond, we sense it won't be long until we do. Anxiety, then, over our most primal need is absent in these places. Life thrives in temperate climates, enriched. The barrenness of rock and rock formation is covered with loam and doused in greenery, and even if it's only seemingly so, this vivification gives everything a pleasant, lethargic lilt. If we don't feel immortal there, life seems sufficiently entrenched to reduce time's urgency, magnifying our own significance and putting us in a reassuring state, making longevity, one of our most prominent pursuits, appear on our side.

The desert produces no such illusion.

I spent maybe eight weeks there over as many years visiting my father, but in certain ways that's enough. The place is immediate. If I was surprised to find such an abundance of life it didn't take long to see how tenuous a hold all of it has. Every species of cactus is a marvel of resilience, but standing next to one, fingering its spines and dried-leather flesh, elicits the sense that life here is adventitious, a corruption of the land's otherwise petrified trance. Organisms seem like they've made a mistake and know it, having blundered into a plane that treats all life like a virus, isolating each form and sieging it with the antibodies of heat, time, and desiccation. No matter how comfortable bottled water, salt pills, and a good map may make us feel here, we absorb the precarious nature of desert life and understand its meaning. It shrivels us, for significance is our everything.

We all want our lives to mean something and most often believe they do, right down to the smallest events. Whether we call it pride, ego, or the sense of self, it's this element of being that supplies our greatest hope. It fortifies, filling us with everything from self-worth to dignity to a sense that what we accomplish will echo beyond our brief lives. Time—and our ability to manipulate its definition—is the key, the skill we use to delude ourselves, making what comes after death at least tolerable. Dying itself, after all, isn't what troubles us, since most people absorb rather well the fact that life ends. It's what comes next that needs tinkering, and we mostly solve this by condensing time. Even those fluent in antiquity or engrossed in future millennia lop off most of either scale when it comes to their personal lives, compacting the earth's chronology around the otherwise infinitesimal span given to us. We may revere Homer, worship the scriptures, or understand the importance of Newton and Locke to the present age. We may stretch our horizons as far out in the future as we can. Still, our sense of self stays out of these forays. Nothing of great import, in other words, seems to extend a generation or two behind or ahead of our own. The memories of a great-grandfather may have significance, but what happened to our ancestors a century and a half ago—even if known—doesn't carry much weight beyond nostalgia. Looking forward, we make great efforts to endow our children and grandchildren a better world, but after that it's too hard to see. Such shaping of time inflates the self and shores up our sense of purpose. Geology, though, is its undoing, and the desert is where geology lies disrobed and unashamed.

Ten minutes after a quick tour of his house, my pop and I climbed a mountain close by. Compared to nearby summits it wasn't more than half a butte, but as a day outside was our only aim it was perfect. The day was like most desert days, cloudless and hot, and pleasant beyond what my now rainforest-hunched shoulders could fully fathom.

We walked through a flat before reaching the ascent, where a half-measure trail switch-backed over and across the slope, rising gradually before increasing sharply halfway up. The rocks were oddly arranged. Huge sandstone boulders were stacked and scattered on the top and down through the middle, while at the bottom rested the smaller cobble and pebbles. Gravity, I thought, might have had it otherwise, but I was new to this place. Saguaros reached their simple arms out over everything and, below these, the furry cholla and stubby barrel cacti scratched out an existence in the sand.

If the country was new to me, our rhythm wasn't. We picked our way up the mountain, sometimes on the trail, sometimes off, with thirty-some years flowing between us. This, I realized, was why I had come, to follow my father like I had through the decades in a host of other landscapes, some familiar, some not. As in all those places, we pointed out plants and bird life to each other, looked for fox scat or coyote sign. We spoke, but in a peripheral dialect, instead judging each other's well-being through inflection and body language. Such assessments are essential. Modern life drifts people about like pollen, but we seek out again and again what's most important in the same way that plants seek sunlight. Such contact, however brief, energizes us, and we again breathe freely. Knowing each other so thoroughly, then, in just a few strides we had affirmed what we needed to affirm.

He explained what he'd learned of ironwood. It grows where the mountain pitches steeply half way up, with each thick, gray branch a whirlwind of snarls, knots, and curves. It lives great lengths of time but never becomes much taller than a man, limited by the scarce sustenance it can coax from the desert. The wood is dense and hard, and we edged through or around each tree while slowly making our way up. Sparrows sang here and there, and a covey of Gambel's Quail buzzed away after our route had pinned them between an ironwood and a pair of egg-shaped boulders.

Once out of the ironwood shade, we walked along a ridge of scattered boulders and fractured bedrock, where just over the first ledge a series of loud, echoing trills descended like a weighted object thrown down a slope. Whatever they were, there were two of them, playing off of one another. My father leaned against a rock. I did the same. He listened, head down. Somewhere he'd heard this before and I knew it would be only a matter of time until it came to him. Meanwhile I waited, enjoying the song. "Canyon Wrens," he finally said, raising his eyes. "I didn't know they came down this low." He'd only seen them once, a pair like this one in a mountain range further north.

The songs continued and we walked around the ridge, hoping to find the birds themselves. The ridge was a false summit and we made our way down a short slope before the land rose again. It was in this dip that we spotted them, calling and skittering about in the jumbled boulders ahead.

There are rare times when it seems that birds put on a show just for you. This was one of them. Unmistakably wrens, they had stout little bodies with an upturned tail, and the brown patterning making up their plumage wasn't far from the Carolina and House Wrens familiar to me from youth, and the winter ones livening Southeast's spruce forests with their boisterous songs. It was their bills, though, that set these desert wrens apart, those and their song. Most wrens have a needle-like beak, but nothing like this. These stretched out further and made a perfect crescent. The birds didn't fly much, only bursting for short stretches from crag to crag, hopping down and up each crack, pausing to probe for crickets and spiders. All the while they spoke to one another in the same series of cascading pitches, monkish in their repetition, un-monkish in their joy. I'd never seen anything like it. At times they'd hop up a boulder then leap off, fluttering and tumbling to the next crevice, singing away. We watched until it ended the way most birding trysts do: too soon. One flew around the scattered boulders and the other followed. We listened, but they were gone.

In large ways we're alone in the world, but it's our attachment to others that makes us significant. We seek out and find a scarce few truly binding companionships and labor freely to maintain them. Memories seal the covenant. Most times a lasting memory is slow to germinate, and the great pleasure is that we rarely remember when it was sown, largely recalling it for the person or people with whom it was shared. Other images, however, imprint right away.

We continued our climb. I felt light. Each wren had a sliver of mottled plumage on the underwing and I traced the pattern in my mind, recording the echoing song while I did. I doubted I'd ever see the same species again but it didn't really matter. We wear intimate memories like a necklace, running our fingers over them, fondling the collection as the old hermits would their relics, as meaning itself. I threaded this one on like a pearl. My father walked ahead and I followed behind, looming the sand between us with Pennsylvania ferns and Connecticut oaks and Alaskan devil's club. We thrive in relationships because we're significant there, and we buttress them with the mortar of new memories, giving us shape.

Deserts, though, can have something else to say, and when we reached the top I heard this voice in full. From most peaks anywhere you look down upon a valley, but this was a vastness, something seemingly without end. It had oceanic qualities in that way, but oceans offer a remedial vista, with their waters shielding the truth beneath it. This gives both the allure of mystery and the womb-ish promise contained in all water. In the desert you just get the truth of time's crushing prowess, blasting every mechanism we use to thwart it. Here you see rock, naked. Across from us a series of broad mountains humped up from the great plain. At a distance the saguaros were still visible at the lower elevations, but each rise was bald, standing there with nothing but cliffs and ledge, plateaus and endless rock.

It's the strata that get you. The rock was sedimentary, sandstone probably, laid down not in days or years, but in epochs. Even at this distance dozens of layers could be seen, frozen into the mountains. They weren't horizontal, as the oceans and rivers and winds had originally settled them, but cockeyed, even vertical. At some point tectonics had driven this land beneath the surface and then popped it out again, stretching and deforming the sediment, compacting it into new forms. Seas came and went as did differing ecologies—temperate, dry, temperate, dry. Snow, as well, had probably covered this land many times, as had brackish water, along with lush, teeming swamps. It was simply in another dry period now, and the life upon it ephemeral. Within bare rock you can see this, even feel it, but you'll never understand it, not really. Humans don't have that temporal capacity, at least beyond an academic purpose. We can't. It would ruin us.

Many religions either started in the desert or gained their strength from it. It's no mystery why. Humans create religion to find meaning, significance, and nowhere is this more needed than a desert, where the dryness, strangled life, and denuded strength of time disembodies any import we may invent. Looking out over the rest of it I tried to see the changes to come—the sea coming back, receding, the mountains going under again, breaking rock, changing it, sending it up anew, rivers washing it all away, lava flowing, and always life dying off and adapting. I tried all of this, to envision it, but couldn't see past the desert before me, which will be like it was now further beyond me than people have been on the earth. It would all change, I knew, but I couldn't see that. I wouldn't see it. We retreat from time like we'd retreat from God. I stood next to my father and, if I could have, would've put a hand through my chest to cradle the canyon wren fluttering away just inside.

A COUPLE OF YEARS LATER, and fresh back from another Arizona visit, I walked the Situk on April Fool's, waiting out a delay to the spring Fish and Game season. I'd been scheduled to fly to Ketchikan to work a smolt project on the Chickamin River, a remote drainage raised in Canada. The Chickamin, though, remained frozen, barring the floatplane we needed to access the estuary-based camp, and I'd taken some of the wait-time for myself.

The snow had finally given way and the Situk, Yakutat's most popular feature, ran high. Up ahead a hummingbird elevated and descended repeatedly amidst church-bell blueberry blossoms, boring its needle bill in and out. Unmindful of my approach, it sucked its nectar with aplomb. The spruce overhead bled what was left of the morning rain into mosses and the witch-finger devil's club. Brown bears wear the trail smooth all summer and fall, seeking sockeye, pinks, and cohos, and fishermen wear it further in pursuit of the same. The hummingbird, a Rufus, let me get within feet, then raised itself out of the bushes, flying to the snow-beaten salmon berry stalks lining the other bank. The bird bounded from one stem to the next, looking for starry pink blossoms that hadn't quite bloomed. Finally it gave up, lifting above the twisting alders before buzzing upstream. I pressed toward the several meadows that hop-scotched the forest where I could better enjoy the sun, but first came to the Oxbow.

After a week of dry desert air, Yakutat's humid chill required re-acclimation. This year, too, we'd visited an even hotter place, far down along the Mexican border, a lush riparian ribbon where cottonwoods green up the San Pedro River. Just a brook by New England standards, the San Pedro pulls in every manner of creature in the otherwise sun-cracked desert. Spending the day walking shady trails, we saw several duck species exploiting beaver ponds we were surprised to find so far south. We also saw what had drawn us down in the first place, vermillion flycatchers. The San Pedro is famous for them, with the males as beaming as their name suggests. We spotted a handful throughout the hours-long walk, perched above the gentle creek or alongside beaver flowages, losing themselves in insect flurries.

"Food does that to you," my dad said. "Normally these guys hide, as no one knows better than they do what that color does to draw predators, especially sharp-shinned and Cooper's hawks."

We'd seen two sharp-shinned's, but that didn't arrest the flycatchers' abandon, which my dad lauded.

"Good for them. Sometimes you have to let it all go."

The Arizona visit had become a time to recap our winters. Mine had been highlighted by a trapping trip on the Situk, a canoe affair that lasted eight snow-slogged days, ending on winter solstice. I'd always wanted to read the King James Bible, and sixteen hours a day in a dark tent allowed for it. My dad asked about the read, then about not seeing anyone for eight days.

"It was seven-and-a-half too long," I said. I was kidding, but not by much.

The trap line itself I divided into two, one upstream and one down, checked on alternate days, with each taking all six hours of daylight plus two more to run. Together, they produced a couple of animals a day, split between pine marten and mink. We'd had a better-than-average mink season at the lake that Thanksgiving, and my dad was pleased that such luck had carried over.

"I camped a few miles up from the estuary," I said. "The bottom of the downstream line ended where the river punched through that oxbow a couple of years ago, where those guys I told you about had been chainsawing."

The Oxbow had indeed changed from my first several years in Yakutat, a change that happened overnight. The way it stood as I looked out after seeing that hummingbird was no longer a bow, but a place that had shortened the river by a tenth of a mile, leaving a dried-up old curve coiled around the spruce peninsula that the flow once circumscribed. Everyone knew high-water would eventually blow it out, and two years before that had finally happened.

A winter storm did it, jumbling hordes of flood-swiped spruce into the gap. Every spring the same two guides had boated the Situk for decades, chainsawing log jams just enough to allow passage, and I happened to be at the Oxbow the day they cleared it. I'd been dog-sitting a couple of labs and, just as I was doing while awaiting the Chickamin to ice-out, I took advantage of the melting snow to drive down to the river and let the dogs run. As they tore through mud and remnant snow on path and off, I heard saw and boat motors a mile away. These were run by Yakutat's foremost guides, Lee and Hank, and I braced for the former's silent suspicions and the latter's congenial jibery.

Over the years I occasionally heard Lee speak, but rarely even half-understood his murmurings. He had a mythology of his own, most of which sounded within earshot of truth. Like most Vietnam veterans, no one other than himself can really say what he did over there, but stories range from more than a few Special Forces tours, to dead-eye sniper abilities, to classified missions across the border. For all I know, he played cards in Da Nang the whole time, but I doubt it. What is known is that he just showed up in Yakutat one day, belted with an enormous knife and quick to throw a punch. He survived a gut stabbing and, according to majority remembrance, beat the stabber senseless. Not long after he arrived, people said, he lived in

Yakutat Bay for three years on an uninhabited island, purging combat memories while thriving on seal meat. Whatever is or isn't true, he had a talent for sport fishing and started guiding, and became particularly known for his steelhead aptitude.

I knew less of Hank, or at least less was whispered of him. If Lee rarely spoke, Hank never stopped, and you didn't really want him to. From what I could tell, he came up from Oregon in his early twenties to work a logging camp and never left, siring some kids while building a new career guiding for bear and fish. He trapped, too, but dropped it when fur prices crashed in the '80s. Clients loved him. He built fires on the banks and told bawdish jokes, and was every bit as adept as Lee at catching his people fish.

My part boss, all friend Gordie came to Yakutat a few years after Hank and Lee. He'd worked the Situk and had more than a few Hank stories. Once, Gordie floated a canoe with another employee, trying to verify chinook abundance. The sky had opened, fouling the count, and rounding a bend they drifted by Hank on a sand spit trying to fan a fading fire while a few guys kept half dry beneath a tarp.

"He was telling the 'Two Tickets to Pittsburgh' joke," Gordie said. "We've all heard it a thousand times, but you'd think Hank invented it, and those guys hung on every word. He was swearing at the dwindling coals the whole time, squatting down, blowing, tossing soaked twigs on, all the while hitting each line just right. Half the reason guys vacation in Alaska is to hide from their wives for a while, and when Hank nailed the punch line he added his own twist, and those guys got every-thing they paid for right there. Me and my partner had to pull the canoe over we were laughing so hard."

The Situk has high banks. With the labs frothing about, and long before I could see either man, I saw a skyward-shooting water flume. It stopped and started with the idle-rev rhythms of a chainsaw, and I knew someone was toiling with a submerged log. I recognized this from smolt camps where, after pitching the wall tents, cutting winter-borne jams comes first. When sawing wood just beneath the surface, the chain's rapid circu-lation jets water ten feet or more, and keeping yourself dry—along with the saw motor—is deft art. Pulled to the unexpected commotion, the dogs paced the bank above, wagging tails and whining for attention from the two men mid-river.

Each had lashed his boat to the considerable impediment, with the needles of twenty or more piled trunks still green. Pre-occupied with the sinker, Lee sawed away, but having seen the dogs Hank looked over. He loved needling govern-ment employees and, though I doubt he considered me a pure breed, he knew where my paychecks came from. As such, he threw up his hands, running saw included.

"Jesus," he shouted. "Don't shoot! We'll trade whiskey for furs!"

I smiled, nodded, then watched. The current had funneled everything into the new gap, packing it tight, and Hank and Lee looked halfway through a barely boat-width lane. Along with swirling sawdust slicks, rounds of spruce bobbed in several eddies. Lee worked a pinch cut, where careless ambition would find the bar hopelessly bound by the pressurized trunk, but he managed it well, and after a few more sprayings half the log slipped around the boat bow, free to find the ocean. Looking up, he saw me. If he nodded I didn't catch it. I never asked him, but assumed he was suspicious of government workers above all others. He filled the saw with mixture and bar oil, then untied the bowline to re-position the deck for another cut. Tying it again, he yanked the saw cord and went at it.

Hank was high on the jam, limbing, sending bower after bower to the current below. Every bit of sixty, likely older, he hopped from trunk to trunk like a panther, never stopping the saw, zipping branches to access bigger wood.

Guys like this befuddle nearly everyone, as no one seems to know what to do with them. Raised in a well-heeled suburb then sent on to college, I'd rubbed shoulders all of my life with people from every political stripe who for some reason assume the world is inherently tame, devoid of primordial danger and meant for the haute and urbane alone. With so many of these well-versed in history, moreover, such delusions are even odder, though there is an explanation, as most of us wish to seal unpleasantness out of our lives, particularly that emanating from our DNA. Confronted with *Calibani* such as Hank and Lee, though, those seals will seep.

Despite such leakage, I've always deeply admired this type, recognizing their role in allowing countless others profound contentedness. Still, such figures do hold up a mirror, and one that doesn't lie. As much American protoplasm, then, as citizens, these people remind us that all the wealth and culture, all the peace and security—the altruism most of all—acquired beneath the nation's name didn't come by refined means. Right or wrong aside, to live in such comfort meant that forests needed razing, sod needed breaking, mines needed blasting, and in the grim world we inherited everything from wolves to bears to Natives needed killing, with the unbound Hank/Lee prototype providing these now deeply unappealing services.

This brand is as unfit for a time card as it is for a boardroom. These were cultural berserkers, a coarse elite that blunted in first, de-fanging wilderness, obsoleting themselves in the process while clearing trails for the economies and cultures to follow. Trappers, traders, fighters, drinkers, prospectors, loggers all, they made possible everything that came after, starting five miles west of Jamestown and Plymouth, then moving on to the Shenandoah and Connecticut River Valleys and through to the Sacramento and the Yukon. From the start no one has been comfortable with them, unsettled, perhaps, by the troubling, unremittable debt they're owed, and discomfited by their often disagreeable manner. Writing in the 1830s, when Ohio set the frontier, James Fenimore Cooper had to elide trapping from Natty Bumppo's skill-set when initial readers—from high culture and low—were too put off.

I came across Hank once in a quieter Situk moment. With his clients waiting ashore, he was anchoring his jet boat just off the launch, in the only low-tide channel deep enough to do so. I'd been to town for weir supplies and was about to push a loaded canoe off upriver. He always ribbed me about paddling rather than motoring, and did so again. Two king salmon, chinook, lay in his boat bottom. Fish and Game had just reduced limits to one per angler to compensate for a poor run, which crippled businesses like Hank's, at least in the short-term.

"Well," he said, looking at the fishes' gold, sun-fading flanks. "I suppose you'll tell us next we'll have to wave pom-poms from the bank as they pass on by."

I smiled, knowing he knew that I had nothing to do with such decisions. Besides, if Lee's reticence was a little unnerving, Hank's couthy barbarism was a hoot. He liked everyone and everyone like him. He returned my smile, adding a wink, but before I could shoot back, for the only time in our many encounters he grew sullen.

"You know, the day I got here," he said, "I could see it coming, but it always seemed far off. Now, though, because I'm older I guess, it feels like it's at the door. You could do about anything you wanted here forty years ago, even twenty. Sure there were rules, but hardly anyone bothered with them. Now, though, you need a permit to take a leak on a tree. In ten years they'll lock me and Lee in a zoo, then rope everything off. The only way you'll get to go in the woods is by following some Forest Service kid around who won't let you step off the trail. Christ, you won't even be able to pick berries. They'll just point in the trees and tell you the Latin names of birds, then put you back on a plane and send you on your way."

I'd never heard him utter a wistful word, nor even antici-pated one, and had no idea what to say, more so since—though he was too nice to mention it, maybe to even think it—I was not unduly considered at least the lip of this tide. He sensed all this, and cut the prophesizing short.

"Well, don't mind me," he said, "I'm just a fossil," then pointed to my readied paddle. "And remember, if you Fish and Game boys ever need someone to teach you how to turn a motor over, I rate by the hour."

I didn't know it paddling upriver, and wouldn't know it for a couple of years, but in reading the King James on that trapping trip I realized that figures such as Hank had been spurned from the first, as least as told in The Bible. Cain, the first urbanite, killed dirt-tilling Abel. Esau, the woodsman, was duped by refined, guile-gifted Jacob. Ishmael, the unfavored, was cast out in the wilderness, and generations later John the Baptist came out of that same wild to have his head cut off. Even God, then, didn't know what to do with such people.

I told my dad that along the San Pedro and he laughed. "That's how it goes, I'm afraid. They came down here I guess too, looking for these desert beavers once they'd eaten them up everywhere else, and now here we are but where are they?"

Now, waiting out the Chickamin with neither dogs nor Hank's and Lee's whinnying saws to mind, I could poke around to see if anything beside a hummingbird was active, particularly past the Oxbow in the first moose-friendly willow brake.

Bear droppings lay spaced along the last of the spruce-shaded trail. Dark and fibrous, they reflected the vegetable-rich diet of spring. I looked down, where sun met shade. A wolf had been here. Four torqued tubes of moose and beaver hair, vole fur and bone fragment, crisscrossed one another in a fresh bear print. The canine's own deep pads had left tracks in the mud where the willow clearing began. By late spring, moose cows range thick along this watershed. Willow growth is lush in the soggy ground and the big animals come here to drop calves, nursing them as best they can on milk and buds. Losses, though, are high. Wolves and bears have their own young to fret, and a thousand generations of knowledge, along with ever keener noses, lead both species to these same broken meadows to sniff out the humid musk of moose placenta and track the easy, weakened feast at its source. I looked up. Five ravens, the Tlingit's myth-makers and the land's carrion-eaters, were perched high in a cottonwood, watching. They, too, knew what played out in this country.

Pulling a water bottle and energy bar from my pack, I listened to a fox sparrow whistle deep in the willows. A ruby-crowned kinglet warbled its own croon atop the spruce wall across the meadow, and after a couple of bites I raised the bottle and drank, relishing cool water.

We're new to this, all of us, even the Hanks and Lees. Whether banished from Eden or evolved from hunting and gathering is irrelevant. Either way, we're a collective eye-blink from integration. There was a time when I wouldn't have fussed much over sparrows or hummingbirds. There was a time when I wouldn't have been alone, but in a band, right here, tight-knit and stitched by kinship. It's no energy bar that would've sustained me, but knowledge, the same knowledge as the wolves and bears. We'd all breathe in, deep, through the nose, scenting words, sentences, orisons. Another breath. There it is, sticky and fresh. We fan out. She's lying down, worn, licking her slick and floundering calf in birthy grasses. The bears are out here, too, and the wolf pack, but we find her first. A couple of quick yips by the discoverer and the rest come running—barefoot, hungry, strong. The mother tries to rise but can't. She's speared and the calf clubbed. Some members cut the animals up while others spread out in the brush, crouching, protecting. We're grateful, and express so in some old, abandoned way.

Divinity, I imagine, meant something else then.

I put the pack back on. A pair of orange-crowned warblers, competitors, had joined the kinglet and sparrow in song. Upstream, over the spruce tops, the sun caught the snow on distant mountains.

I enjoyed this, I knew, all of it, and was comfortable, even deeply moved, in these places—forest, desert, anywhere—but didn't belong. None of us do. That world is gone, the language lost. I'd been seeking those words and that God, any God, for so long that I wondered if most of life hadn't slipped elsewhere. In February I'd turned thirty-nine. From an early age I simply assumed that a wife and kids were just around the corner, but so far nothing had stuck, relationship-wise. My mom's eyes had never left me, hospitalized, dying but not dead. She'd always exhorted me to marry, but her valedictory quip about the tethers such commitments require, followed by that "Go forth awhile" gaze, had blotted those appeals. There was too much of the world to know, too much to find, and I probably never thought marriage and fatherhood contained it, but looking off the Situk's bank into moving water I felt something new, a pinprick lament that such scenes and such silence might remain my only venue.

IN MOST CASES, of course, certainly mine to that point, remaining childless is the result of choices made and not made, and any regrets I may have had were nothing rightfully dwelt upon. Persistently piqued by God and the afterlife from an early age, I'd largely lived a head-in-the-clouds life, letting more than a few promising relationships dissolve within that mist. Besides, a Yakutat permanency was beginning to form. Gordie was soon to retire, and with the remote town a tough Fish-and-Game slot to fill, I was slated to take his place despite lacking an academic background in biology. A good job, then, likely for life, in a place I adored, was no future to complain about. That fall, however, another pang, far deeper, unsettled me in places where I didn't care to be unsettled, this one a simple consequence of being born.

My father was getting old. Such recognition was at last impossible to ignore, something I finally acknowledged on a duck hunt that October. I obviously understood that he'd die, but always assumed it would be something sudden. As a kid, for instance, I trembled each time he traveled for work that a car wreck or plane crash would snatch him, but a long, smokeless goodbye never crossed my mind.

My dad never tired, never stumbled, never seemed awkward in the field. This had always been so and I never considered it would be otherwise. When my sisters and I were children he'd take us for long hikes through pathless woods, lifting us up on tireless shoulders when the brush was too thick or the day too long. By that autumn in Yakutat, I'd hunted with him for thirty years, and in all that time his spryness never flagged. He shadowed through landscapes at sixty-five the same as he had at forty. Everyone occasionally falls, of course, and he took some true tumbles off of logs or down snowy slopes, but he always popped up, brushing leaves or flakes off like a base-stealer ready to take the next bag.

When something doesn't change, when it seems constant, you never question it nor think to do so. No one walks out at night and wonders if the Big Dipper will look like a deep pot with a long handle. It just does. Humans aren't constellations, though, and even when slow to form, the changes that occur can be quite sudden to the eye. Inevitably, my father's fluidity slipped, and if I once paired his immortality with a retiring thrush, the reciprocal impress came through a water ouzel's song.

He had been slowing. I guess there were signs, but most were too subtle to overthrow the disavowal we erect against the degeneration of those we love, a partition meant to emotively blind us to coming loss. For me, that wall went up at twenty-two while walking a moonlit Pennsylvania creek, a barrier I never even peaked over until duck hunting the upper Situk seventeen years later, when it was razed as quickly as it had been put up.

That first shock came at night. Spurred by the same Huck Finnery that nudged my dad to set Smiley Slater's portion of the Starrucca, we had a few mink sets where beavers had dammed a smaller creek, with the pond forty yards off the road through a hemlock stand. Unposted and out of sight of any house, we went with the it's-easier-to-apologize-than-ask-permission maxim and put in a dozen traps. A few were below the dam in shallow water, and as muskrat sign was thick we decided to run the sets both by day and again around midnight.

With the hour so late and the clay byway so little traveled, we abandoned the drop-off plan and checked together. A front had come in, layering inches of snow, followed by a temperature drop to near zero, which left both the trees and the looming beaver dam glittering in moon-laced snow and ice. With the first set near and likely frozen, I gripped a hatchet, looking up the well-lit, iced-up current for animal movement, trapped or otherwise, and not paying attention to my father behind me. A thump changed that.

I was used to an occasional spill, but his helplessness here was a first. I stood dumb. An ice patch must have taken him, but instead of jumping up, he floundered about, pawing the snow in something like panic while an intermittent hand or foot slipped away from him.

"Mike," he said. "I need help."

This wasn't how it worked. I rode on his shoulders, he picked me up out of tall ferns, even sat next to me by fire when I was too adolescent-punchy to understand that was exactly what I wanted, what I needed. He re-iterated.

"Please, Mike. I need help. I can't see. My glasses are gone."

From shock I nearly laughed, then recovered. He has lousy vision, scarcely able to see more than a few inches with a naked eye. The moon caught both lenses where they lay two feet from a groping hand.

"Don't move," I said, then stepped forward, reaching down. Brushing snow off, I held the glasses before him, then helped him up.

"Thanks," he said.

That was it. If St. Paul had dropped from a hemlock to sledgehammer my forehead it would have had less effect. Though my dad was far from being old, I'd seen that day coming and wasn't prepared. Up went the wall, which did its job flawlessly until I was thirty-nine and he was sixty-nine.

Though I'm sure in the preceding years he was increasingly stiffer, harder of hearing, slower to react, I didn't allow myself to see it. Now, though, it was obvious. We hunted out of a canoe for the first couple of days and I had to hold the gunnels firm as he labored in and out. For thirty years I knew him to be an early riser and quick out the door, but that changed, too. For ducks, the best hunting comes at first light. We were getting out long after this. Fortunately, the actual shooting is secondary to our enjoyment, so little was missed. It was just a different pace, one undoubtedly linked with age. My own limbs were kinked up a bit in the mornings as well, though, so I still failed to acknowledge it, this onset of my father's mortality. The next day, however, when we hunted by foot, the illusion vaporized, with an unlikely antidote mitigating that void.

A river's relation to the ocean isn't unlike that of a human being's to dying. For each, the beginning is blessed ignorance. Infants are unencumbered with thoughts of death and rivers have their source in springs, welling up from the earth without any knowledge of the ocean's oblivion. Most rivers start at elevation, and as the springs combine to form a single flow they tumble down through rocks and ravines with abandon. We behave likewise. Children have a general understanding of death, but not their own, and go at life recklessly. Maturity creeps in during adolescence, instilling just the barest hint of caution, since death is no longer a detached fantasy. Rivers mature as well, still coursing at a fair clip but tempered now as the elevation eases. They also broaden. Swelled by tributaries, the waters seek to expand, probing as much of the world as they can while in their prime. Humans, too, carve similar channels of expansion, acquiring knowledge and experience. Soon, though, something happens in both rivers and people. Each passes its midway point, and an end can be felt in earnest. Rivers slow, seeming to sense the ocean ahead. They bend and twist, lengthening their course, often running parallel with the beach to ward off the salting tides, while humans, too, slow themselves, braiding and meandering, ox-bowing, anything to delay their own end. The difference, naturally, is that rivers are constantly replenished whereas people just die, and know it.

The Situk is short, twenty miles all in, rising from two mountain-fed lakes. If the river brings Yakutat some fame as a sport-fishing mecca, all of it is concentrated in the thirteen and a half miles below the lone bridge crossing it, called Nine Mile for its distance from town. Scarcely a soul knows the upper reaches, but mallards pour in every October for salmon eggs. Once the sockeye have spawned in the lakes and the pinks have horded the entire river, cohos—from late August through Halloween—mostly use the above-bridge waters to spawn. The ducks know this and have developed a taste for the coho's caviar. Eagle-wary, they paddle out from the eddies, dipping their long necks below the surface, sifting gravel for spawn.

Hunting from the canoe had been slow, so I took my dad to Nine Mile. Bear trails run down each bank, making it a feasible place to jump shoot. With his love of grouse hunting I thought the walking would be preferable, but that was working from memory.

The bear trails here follow the river's edges. Trees are mostly Sitka Spruce, held by roots running parallel with thin topsoil. Glacial gravel lies underneath. The trunks are highly vulnerable to wind, and blow-downs crisscross the pathways. Bears walk over and under them with ease, but to people they're an obstacle. I'd seen my dad hurdle wind-blown oaks or tear through sheaves of brambles on his way to a downed grouse, but now each log was a chore. He'd put a hand on them, gaze down, then look up at me. I took his gun, holding an arm out so he could steady himself as he tottered over. His aim hadn't suffered, and he shot a couple of mallards. They tumbled into the brush, where I expected him as always to scramble for the retrieval. He didn't. His mind, I knew, did, but his body just shuffled forth, and I'd bring the duck back. In important ways I felt fulfilled, able to repay at least some of an owed debt. In others I was horrified, for the first time sensing with visceral certainty the bereavement to come. Any defenses I had to thwart this feeling combusted, and in that light I saw myself. Like him, my father, I'd wear down with age, coming to assess mortality in the same crippling proximity. To know you're going to die is one thing, but to feel it, to see it through your own blood, is something else. We all know that people can in part relive their lives through their children, but few consider what kids can see ahead through their parents.

You use the tools at hand. Living is rife with natural shocks and we employ what means we're given to restore equilibrium. I was given a water ouzel.

No one calls them water ouzels, but instead use the collo-quial *dippers*. Prior to Yakutat I'd only seen a few, and those in the Colorado Rockies. My dad and I visited my sister there a few times, attempting the local habit of winter fly-fishing along the Roaring Fork and Frying Pan Rivers where, among other pleasant experiences, we watched the goofy gray birds slipping in and out of frigid currents.

Dippers are a quirk. They look like several species, behave like a few others, but for the most part are a unique entity.

They're solitary to slightly social by nature, and can best be described—looks-wise—as a cross between a catbird and a house wren. Their tails resemble the upturned variety of the wrens, and they're the exact cinder-gray of the catbird.

They're probably called dippers for two reasons, with the most prominent being their hunting technique. They hop and fritter about stream-side stones, alone or in pairs, dipping into the current where they pluck mayflies, caddis, and other nymphs from the rocks. Climbing back out, they then bop, or dip, in the manner of phoebes. Normally quiet but curious, dippers spend most of their time in and around these small, rocky streams, feeding upon the same larval life as the trout and salmon young who live there, going after the nymphs that spend their lives either upside down beneath rocks or crawling upright atop them.

For the most part you have to look for dippers if you want to see them. Where they exist, they're a companion to fishermen and backpackers, but tend to stay clear of most other human traffic. This isn't conscious, though, as when you do see them, they don't seem terribly upset by your presence. I was delighted to find them in Alaska.

We made it upriver about a mile and a half before turning back. Toward the end we came to a particularly large log. I could tell my dad was tired, but going around this one would have been equally challenging given the nearby patches of thorny devil's club. The trunk was tall and thick and I straddled it like a horse. I put the guns on the other side and held out a forearm. He placed a hand near my elbow and the other atop the log, then paused. The stream coursed by and from it came music I'd never heard. We say 'birdsong' but even the most lyrical ones don't match our ear for melody, not really. This one, though, did. I looked over, locating the rock-perched bird amidst the murmuring water. My dad failed to get his leg up but succeeded a second time, now drawing on my arm to hoist the rest. I pulled, helping, but focused on the bird.

It was a dipper, perched on a log. I'd heard them, but never in this context. The dipper's song is among the best-kept secrets in the birding world, yet here notes poured from its open throat like gospel, and its eyes moved around, seeking audience. October isn't breeding season, but rather when winter ruffles its bony fingers through the woods, setting mood. This bird, then, was simply enjoying itself. There couldn't be another reason.

Like all creatures, dippers live tough, meager lives. This one was feeding on abundant salmon eggs, but mostly theirs is a scant undertaking, breasting chilled waters to roust up enough bug life for another day. Still, this creature spilled over with pleasure. Whatever pain and anxiety runs through our lives, life itself overwhelms it. The dipper knew that, and now I did too. My father and I were both aware that day that we wouldn't have this forever—there was no need to say it—but we'd had it for nearly forty years and would have more for as long as it lasted, and just then that was enough. He'd be gone someday, I'd lose him, but salmon were in the stream right now and the weight of fat mallards hung from my neck. A dipper, too, was singing, and I could take my father's hands in my own and let him down gently off a log. If I was no longer blind, for the moment neither of us could see the tidewaters ahead, though not even that palliating melody could flush the brine from my nostrils.

ANEW

My long two-pointed ladder's sticking through a tree
Toward heaven still,
And there's a barrel that I didn't fill
Beside it, and there may be two or three
Apples I didn't pick upon some bough.
But I am done with apple-picking now.

—ROBERT FROST

Even with the recognition that my father was ageing, however, or the nibbling notion that I might remain childless, Yakutat grew ever more comfortable. I'd dubbed it Whoville, the Seuss-borne place where happiness reigns, and nearly from the beginning, ten years now, it had been far more home than holiday.

Regarding children, too, something had come up, or at least may have come up. Two Decembers before, on the annual visit to my sister's family in Connecticut, I'd met Karen. We were both seeing people at the time, but two years later—a few months after the dipper hunt—she emailed. Neither of us had forgotten the connection and, both single again, we worked to splice two wildly divergent lives, geographically and otherwise, initially finding a simple if brief solution.

I'd been scheduled to attend a conference in Maine the last week of June, and Karen made arrangements to join me. For years my father had joked that such forays would make "just another chapter," but while the beginning of any relationship feels different, this one felt more so. Each of us forty, having both lived free-radical romantic lives, we knew what lay ahead if we didn't abandon old, fruitless habits.

"Well," Karen said at dinner the second night, "we both know the tune. We can either date by distance before someone opts out, or I can freeze what eggs I have left on the chance we decide it'll work in a couple of years. Or we can just get this started."

Sometimes you let it all go. Like the midge-giddy vermillion flycatchers, Karen and I did likewise, generating far different sensations when I boarded the plane back to Alaska then I'd ever felt. Still, I had a pleasant life and a pleasant job to return to, with no reason to believe I wouldn't be enjoying both for years to come.

July was sockeye month. Salmon are punctual and we scheduled surveys according to historical run times. The day had come for the first Sockeye Creek count, a skinny riffle-and-pool affair running beneath canopy spruce. It was my favorite, a ten-mile brush-beat roundtrip.

I pulled the gray pickup off the town intersection toward Harlequin Lake, an enormous glacial body where the thirty mile road ends. I wouldn't make it that far, with the creek cutting under at mile twenty-two. It was early enough that they hadn't begun burning at the dump, and the usual skein of pungent smoke that lay across the road was absent. A dump bear, one of the young boars, loped out of the alders and crossed in front, eager for the day's alms—everything from wax fish boxes to peanut butter jars to disposable diapers. I slowed, watched him disappear into dense young spruce, then accelerated into the day.

It hadn't rained for two weeks—worrisome in a rain-forest—and the dust rose up behind me like a locust cloud. For the first few miles the plant life was thick but short—alder and fireweed reclaiming clear-cuts, basking in the moment before the spruce starts shaded them out. The old stumps, ashen and blanched, twenty to forty years gone from living organism, stood mute above the growth like the graves they were, stretching a hundred thousand or more in the neat-boxed lines of each cut. Out on the root of an over-turned stump, the sunlight quivered in the purple-black of a perched raven. Head cocked, it watched another of its kind carve circles over recovering ground. Seeing the flyer had spotted nothing, the stationary one stepped off the root, drifting on the power of a few wing flaps in its partner's wake.

Another mile gone. Two. Then three. One more.

Wildflowers adore roadsides. The Transportation Department mows ten yards off either side every summer, allowing flowers to thrive. Back on the beach the lupines were already dropping petals, but bloom is delayed further inland. Thousands of vedettes, then—stoutly mailed, purple and white—lined each shoulder, the tips of most still a clenched cap. Beneath them, spearish paintbrush leaves coned from the grass, pending their yellows and scarlets and terra cottas for another day. A riff of potholes pocked the road ahead and, as I slowed, a Varied Thrush, fledgling fuzz eeling from stunted feathers, skipped twice out of the lupines, taking shaky flight across the road.

Yakutat has one radio station, broadcast through a phone out of Sitka. I flicked it on. The news brief. Preparations for hurricane season down south. Economic indicators, most weak. An ethanol debate, a proposed bill. Adultery. Four soldiers killed in Afghanistan. Local stuff, the fisheries reports. I turned it off. We forget what pleasure driving is. With the engine humming to the *diktat* of your own volition, the past and present often dissipate in the backdraft, and you seem to speed by the future fast enough not to care too much about it. Twenty-two miles, though, doesn't last long and, reaching the appointed spot, I pulled onto the shoulder where the creek passes beneath through four separate culverts.

Few summer days hit seventy degrees on the Forelands, but this one was seventy-five, and already sweat dampened my thinning hair. Reaching behind the front seat, I slid the rifle out and put three rounds in the clip, then tucked three more in an easy-to-reach pocket. My daypack held a water bottle, lunch, and a rain jacket as, sun or no sun, you never forget rain gear. The only other items were the clickers—the fish-counters— simple metal devices with a tab that rolled white numbers on a black backdrop whenever pressed, similar to what an umpire uses to count balls and strikes. There were two, tied to either end of a small cord draped around my neck. That was it. I crossed the road, slipped through the salmon berry and alder screen concealing the creek, then billy-goated down the third culvert into burbling water.

If you're looking for split-second majesty, Sockeye Creek isn't much to see. The land is flat and tree-shrouded. No Half-Dome rises here. No Grand Canyon sinks nor Old Faithful spews nor Bering Glacier churns. No God on the half-shell. In a few spots I could jump across it, and for most of its length it runs no more than five yards wide, never going above my head except at the sickle pond, a crescent-shaped water body that the creek both feeds and drains. You have to walk this place, sitting from time to time, watching.

Do it enough, learn it by years and seasons, and the old questions seep through like mist.

This was the first count here, the first of three—two for sockeye, one for coho. Sockeye wouldn't be spawning now, or at least very few, but there always seemed to be an early pair just above the first culvert. I looked right and there they were, tanager-red, steadied head-first in the murmuring current just outside the undercut spruce roots. The male dipped its anterior and quivered, routing a puff of sand. I watched him drift a few feet and re-settle. The creek is a bit odd for this country. It runs through a series of eskers, hill-like mounds left by sub-surface glacial melt. Each of these hummocks contains ice-dumped rock deposits that have scattered along the stream bed over the years, making this bed more stable than most of the Forelands, which is comprised of smaller-grade gravel. These two fish were pushing the same rock chunks I'd seen their ancestors move for the last ten years. With a copper-green head, rich red

187

body, and a hook, or kype, developing the length of its upper jaw, the male showed little of the wear that would come with earnest nest construction, depressions in the stream bottom known as redds. Similarly colored but with a more shapely head, the female held next to him. Her belly neither soft nor sagging, she had a ways to go. If an eagle or an otter or a bear or a wolf took one or the other, partners by the hundreds would arrive soon enough. One clicker denoted single fish, the other groups of ten for the pools where hundreds sometimes held and estimates were made. I cusped the counter dangling over my right shoulder—the singles—and pressed twice.

Without much spawning activity, this earlier count found fish in only a handful of pools, one just fifty yards from the road. I adjusted the rifle strap on my shoulder, then walked a dry, normally-wet gravel bar. The creek was as low as I'd seen it. Spruce mix heavily with hemlock this far into the Forelands, each ranging to equal heights, a lattice of sun-sifting needle-work. Though occasional gaps produce unblemished light, you mostly walk through fenestrated shadow. I crossed the old, rotting windfall in such a mix—the first of a hundred or more—sliding one leg over, then the other. At the top of the riffle I cheated left where the schooled fish—remnants of horrific attrition—were easily herded in the ensuing pool. A smaller bunch than normal, I clicked them off.

If I couldn't have walked this creek blind-folded by now, I probably could have come close. High-water events had left generations of spruce tangled in jams and crisscrossing the current along its length, and I worked my way up, over, and

under the slip-throughs and catwalks that I always had, tabbing
fish. With no sockeye in a normally reliable pool, I cut across
the bare gravel hemming it, noting a shred of rapidly drying
milt—torn, buff-white, marred with a spider-burst of rotting
blood—stuck to the stones, a lone vestige the mink and jays
hadn't scavenged from a bear kill. With the sun muscling
between evergreens I moved through cylindrical light, recalling
a near lifelong, ambient mindset that had been jeopardized
only days before along Maine's rocky coast. Though that same
frame of mind had run unchallenged for twenty-five years, I'd
never really been aware that such a continuum existed, only
realizing the previous October where it had started and what
exactly it had been.

Not long after my dad had left following the upper Situk
hunt, I'd been flown fifty miles south to carcass sample sockeyes on the East River, a short, clear-water stream whose delta
nearly abuts the Alsek's, an enormous glacial torrent popular
with commercial fishermen and summer rafters. The trip was
an annual affair, one to gather spent spawners and to pluck
scales for ageing purposes. I surveyed the river weekly by air
June through August, and spent a night on the Alsek each week
to monitor the fishery there, but this fall trip was the only
appreciable time I spent on the East every year. A three-mile,
lake-like river, it was left by recently evacuated glaciers now
dwindled high in the Brabazon Range, and by October, apart
from a couple of bear camps, the place was mine.

The biologists required six-hundred fish, which depending
on weather and run strength took two, maybe three days. Near

the end of the second afternoon I slipped three dozen fuzzy corpses off of a wire, laying them on the well-tramped bank grass where brown bears traffic all month to pack winter fuel away. The sample cycles were all the same—wade, find fish, spread them out, pick scales, take data—and this bunch would make six hundred.

The shotgun I propped fast by in a willow fork. As Gordie had advised, I'd learned to make noise, and with no people around used these annual days to hunt ducks, with the occasional gun blasts providing all but the edgiest bears ample warning. Alongside the fish I'd laid a single wigeon, a flavorful if smaller duck, and was hoping for one more to make a decent meal. Taking data sheets, tweezers, and a cloth measuring tape from a dry bag, I kneeled, scraping the custard-mold fungus off the first fish's side. By October the sun doesn't have much punch, but even as it snuck below the cottonwood tips across the calm water behind me, it bestowed welcome warmth. Half way through the second fish row I straightened, stretching, then upon the sound of swarming wings grabbed the gun and turned, as quickly unshouldering to let the forty bufflehead through.

More bee than bird, bufflehead aren't great table ducks, but are spectacular on the wing and to the eye, at least the white-pated males. These intended to land but, seeing me, resumed full flight. They're named for their outsized heads, or buffalo heads, and their tight, stubbed wings allow tremendous dexterity. Framed in mist and cottonwood, all were about to pass twenty yards out front, but as occasionally happens one drake broke off, dipping below the deciduous crowns right for me, lighting its wings. Three feet off the deck the pink feet lowered, toes spread for the long skid, while the sun breached the diaphanous webbing between each digit. Spotting me, the bird at last understood, regaining altitude to catch its mates, but that was enough. I'd careened back to Pennsylvania, to being fourteen years old on the Starrucca, finally recognizing the significance of that portal I'd slipped through along Smiley Slater's summertime river.

"Christ," I thought, watching the little ducks peel toward the East's mainsprings. "I guess that was it."

Though persistently needled with doubt, and with all the terrors of annihilation attending it, I realized it had never occurred to me that there isn't a God, not really, but until those sun-tinted, roseate duck feet, I'd never understood that I'd dedicated my life to that aim, to the unflagging pursuit of divine definition: form, character, intent, purpose—all of it. In the vein-work mapping the tissue between those tined toes, I understood equally that an amble along a modest creek bed four-thousand miles and twenty-five years off had embarked that quest, for if empiricists walk the woods perceiving data, to me the place had always been the dashed-off bioglyph through which murmurs the source. Life's complexity and delicate fortitudes, its kaleidoscopic intellect and stolid persistence, couldn't possibly be the product of chance, and unable to subordinate this creationist intuition to the notion that all came without purpose from a minor explosion, such evanescence had left me a rabbit-less hound—scent-riled, water-parched, briar-torn. If unsure of what brought us here, though, or what its motives might have been, the chase had been all, and since witnessing that hellgrammite's lacey lungs fronding creek water, or those five wood ducks take flight, or my own blood unable to clot due to a parasite's molecular subterfuge on the barefoot walk home, everything—love, family, evil, friendship, altruism, suffering, nature, everything—had been refracted through that seeking. Now, over half my life later, with those bufflehead flocking off, I knew that it always would. Equally, however, I realized that this made me someone incapable of doing what nearly everyone does, of shucking our inherent childhood wonder the way pupae shed initial integuments.

Standing on the East's banks just then, I didn't care. Months later, Maine changed that. In spending time with Karen, along with my first earnest paternal drive, such insouciance had been thrown into question, an inquiry that hadn't at all abated two miles up Sockeye Creek.

I slipped the rifle strap from my shoulder, dipped beneath a stubby spruce trunk, then re-harnessed the weapon before slogging through knee-deep water, scanning undercut banks for fish. A clipped chirp and a bit of motion foiled the stillness. A winter wren—tail erect—hopped and fluttered among some washed out spruce roots, searching stony interstices for food. Tiny and brown, etched with delicate barring like the cactus-hunting canyon wrens, this one was quiet save for a chirp or two, a contrast to March when they return the forest to spring with trilling fusillades.

I clicked off another pair of spawners, early arrivals who, unlike the first two, were more a vestige of life. The rich, arterial red had drained to a pale hint, and both fins and tails were frayed to spiny, wax-yellow bones. With each thinned from ejaculation, they held upright more out of habit now than will, and only the half-fallen hemlock overhead kept the eagles from finishing them off. Soon they'd drift downstream, dead, either to be plucked from the water or to settle in a gentle pool where the nymphs, worms, and juvenile coho would reduce them to sediment.

Coming to a large wind throw, I straddled one leg on each side and laid the rifle on decaying wood. Tiny mushrooms, filaments of them with dew-drop heads, black in the stem and orange at the tip, were clustered in front of the gun. I had no idea what they were called, only that above the gurgling waters their delicacy of form belied a rapine for what the old tree still retained. For all its elegance, life's every cell is complicit in a feral symbiosis, and if I was taken by the mushrooms' frail splendor, it wasn't lost on me that similar fruiting bodies had been devouring this tree long before it had toppled.

Picking the rifle up I bent forward, splaying along the log to look down the barrel. The sights were clear, and I sat up. An old gun, it had been hard-used. Chips of various ages marked the butt and fore grip—a few of which were my own doing— and rust had been blued over and again. The action, though, was true. I unlocked the bolt, then re-engaged before ejecting the chambered round and snatching it with the same hand. Unlocking the magazine, I let the two remaining shells tumble into my palm. All well, and I reloaded. Some creeks were more bear-heavy than others, and this was one of them.

A sockeye finned in the pool above, then another. Still sitting, I ran a hand across my head, pressing sweat. July. Birdsong declines, but a fox sparrow husked a few notes from the salmon berries across the creek, lacking the lustful declaration of a few weeks before, while below, caddis larvae moved about the stream bottom inside the makeshift pebble tubes meant for self-protection, their bent, mechanical legs dragging them forward. Downstream, a dipper, this one silent, dropped off a rock and entered the water. Emerging, it gained another stone, extracted a larva from its dwelling, then swallowed. Nature seems so peaceful at times that we believe it to be so, and I wondered if joy wasn't life's only say, the rebellion against all that we—from people to buntings to tadpoles to stoneflies—don't see, and may never comprehend.

Standing, I resumed the count, clicking off the few sockeyes in the pool above before walking on. Some stretches were clean, not many fish and not many blow-downs, while others were choked with both. I came to the drowned forest where the channel had shifted some time ago, inundating trees in one line of wood while leaving the old route dry. The mountains, miles away, were visible here. The creek bed opens the forest in such a manner that a graveled, timberless draw can be seen between two ridges. The slopes face south, and every year the same melt pattern lingers in the shadiest joint they share, one vertical line intersected by a shorter near the top. This cross clings through mid-July, and I looked upon it. Pure white save round the edges, where the earth's heat and burning sun ate away, a run-off channel below it ran turgid, carrying snow and flecks of mountain downslope. Standing there, in the jostled creek bed, with the peaks deliquescing in the distance, you can rightfully amend the old haiku: *Though the capital may fall, the mountains and rivers remain.* At least for a time.

When I reached the sickle pond I hadn't seen a fish in half a mile. In their urgencies, sockeye wipe the algae in the shallower riffles clean—even a few fish—and the wavy green fuzz clinging to such spots told me that I wouldn't see another salmon. Counts, though, are made between fixed points, so I'd continue through to the end, enjoying the sunshine.

The pond opens in full. The forest behind it gives way to muskeg, in this instance a spongy morass of glacial refugia, a place the big ice danced around on its last advance, leaving remnant species found nowhere else on the Forelands—lodgepole pine, northern pike, a distant relative of the crab apple. The pond itself is a sharp crescent that Sockeye Creek enters near the east-most point and then runs out at the tip of the same. I walked into unopposed sun, wading the deep channel to access the inlet's open gravel.

This was the early count, but at least a few fish were usually here, ripening. Some years they stacked so thick that by late July the pond muddied too much for a proper count, and only a rough estimate was possible. I stood at the water's edge while the creek behind me whispered its diminished strength. A few tree swallows coursed above the water, nipping the surface from time to time. The sun had triggered a hatch, and midges found their way from water to air. In places, in the trim between spruce and meadow, elderberry grew in woven bunches, its blossoms filling the atmosphere with a faint, skunk-like odor. All along the short beach, bleached salmon relics, translucent, lay scattered among gray broken stone. Gill plates and ribs, a few jaw lines. Sockeye, pink, and coho. The valley of dry bones. When alive here, sockeye always rested where the inlet feeds the pond and, with hands cupped about my eyes, I scanned for red forms. Nothing.

Squatting, I laid down the rifle, then bowled my hands to splash my face. Through the water below thick green algae patched the clay floor, while across the pond a tribe of monkshood grew from the sedge, their purple, downward frailty veiling the poison inside. A salmon berry stalk drooped nearby, weighted by a dozen fruits hung over the water. Rosy on top, green-revolving-to-red on bottom, the pimpled berries absorbed the sun, tempting bears, birds, and people. It starts with plant life, all of it, while plant life starts with that unfathomably far off solar fission, and I realized that this was probably as close as I'd come. In all that searching, in all that God-crazed, purpose-crazed hounding that had slow-cooked most of my life, I wasn't sure if I'd found anything at all, only doubting if we've ever really improved on truths we knew from the beginning, that the sun breeds maggots in a dead dog after all.

Piercing and persistent, a familiar sound cut the air. I stood. Not many birdsongs are unwelcome, but the monotone screech of a Lesser Yellowlegs is one of them. They stand atop dying evergreens alongside wetlands, scourging all comers with their well-developed alarum. This one, though, was hurt. Large for a shorebird, they're otherwise unremarkable, with a needle bill, plump body, and stilted legs. Such a one now circled the patch of marsh that led from pond to muskeg. Normally their legs stick straight behind, but here an appendage dangled below in sad inutility. Stammering its protests downward in atonal succession, the bird ascended with each circumference, as if it could out-wing its fate, but it was no matter. It looked to the grass below, circling the circle of its own demise.

The swallows just then were as pleased with their lot as the shorebird was agitated by its own. Many more had gathered to revel in the reap of midge-life. They twittered about, arcing and slicing, intercepting the insects' uncertain careers. Rise and descent, rise and descent, filling themselves with food. Like a dipper's song, you understand joy when you see it as much as you do in hearing it, and as the swallows continued snapping midges from the air I sensed it as well, rising up to the burning blue, all but asking: "Was this it, Master? Was this what you meant to say?"

That was about the last of Yakutat I remember. Karen called the next day, catching me just before I left the bunkhouse for work. She nearly didn't have to say it. Despite the odds our age promoted, we'd both had the same premonition.

"I think I'm pregnant."

"I think so too, just don't ask why I think that."

We laughed, knowing that we'd joke for the rest of our lives that Shannon's was a planned pregnancy—but only if the minutes between salad and an appetizer define a blue-print. After that, life was nothing but fast. The next day she confirmed, and I went to the office to give a shocked but understanding Gordie two weeks' notice.

"Jesus," he said. "So much for retirement."

The call to Arizona was next. For most of my adult life I knew without his saying it that my dad never understood why I didn't yet have kids, why, for that matter, my relationships—oftentimes even the thought of one—had been such hot-potato affairs. I couldn't tell him because I didn't know either, but somewhere in the last couple of years I'd sensed he'd become incurious. He'd retired, and with me single we were able to maintain our Pennsylvania trapping week while starting the new traditions of duck hunting Alaska and walking Arizona. If taken aback, however, any unease he might have had dissolved in seconds, though he assuredly understood long before I did that such news would abruptly end those three weeks, time that had largely come to define us.

"Congratulations," he said. "For God's sake. Congratulations."

Beyond that it was just killing off another pay period while trying to apprehend what was happening, attempting to raze an old mindset to make room for the new. I sold my rifle and shotgun, along with a few other items such as a gillnet and pressure cooker, then studied what finances I'd put away with more vigor than I ever had before. At last the day came, and after a final twilit beach party with friends and co-workers, I caught the plane the next morning and was gone. To Queens. Queens, New York.

Though our advanced years justified it, Karen and I had behaved more like teenagers than forty-year olds, and not long after I landed that spontaneity came to collect. We barely knew each other, and within days, if not hours, understood that. Groping hastily to find a job of some sort, I additionally groped to fathom Karen, and she me. For most of my life men and women seemed to be circles of identical circumference. Something—God maybe—tried to overlay them, a perfect match, but missed, if only slightly. All that shared ground, then, so much common interest, but within those outlying penumbras lay all the fodder for our finest novels, along with the madness of women and men. I told Karen that a few months in, and it may have helped.

"That sounds about right," she said. "Too bad we didn't think of that in Maine."

Through that initial whirlwind we could nearly always make each other laugh. If it wasn't the bridge we needed, it at least made a reliable cofferdam. Two other factors, both critical, helped to seal out our terrors of each other and the specter of unity that otherwise might have scuttled us. Foremost was Shannon, the being steadily levying Karen's womb. Though we didn't announce it, we named her long before her birth. Karen is Irish pride, little more, while I adore rivers, and with the River Shannon the Old Country's longest and most storied, the choice was no choice at all.

Second was family. We both came from strong ones and, with that background at our heels, were each far too wary to break ranks. Besides, deference to tradition wasn't all of it, or even half, but what that tradition provided. With each of us having benefited greatly from in-house parents, we shared a pious desire to do what we could for our own kid, whatever that might cost our respective notions of independence. As is common to many people, a baby made us grow up.

Oddly, what became known as the Great Recession provided a break, or at least a simplification in our domestic options. Dog-shocking, fish-counting, and amateur theologizing wouldn't make an attractive resume anywhere, even in the best of times, let alone in New York City during the dourest economy that all but eighty-five-year-olds could remember. Though I scraped up what temp work I could during the pregnancy—everything from mailroom help to off-the-books day laboring to a two-month stint as a receptionist—it was clear to both of us that Karen's well-developed Human Resources career would be our meal ticket, while I would become whatever I would become to our fast-approaching child. That day came in March, and we entered the parental cyclone, where time both gallops apace and halts at once, a phenomenon for which we had no reference.

"Get ready," a friend of Karen's warned. "They're long days, short months, and shorter years."

She was right. Tuesday afternoon never ended, but soon we woke to find that Shannon was three months old, now six, then eight. For reasons we wouldn't understand for a couple of years, she was a terrifically difficult baby, and nights were spent taking turns walking her around, bobbing her, quickly realizing that little but motion—constant motion—gave her peace. Towards August, too, we concluded that Queens wouldn't do, nor any large city. This was as an abrupt a jolt for Karen as the move from Yakutat had been for me. She'd spent most of her adult life in New York, along with four years in Dublin, but an afternoon with a soon-to-crawl Shannon had her job searching that night.

"Where do you put her down?" she asked. "There's no grass. I never noticed that before."

She'd spent some time as a kid in Rhode Island's South County, where an aunt and uncle still owned a beach house. Her memories were fond, and she applied to a job in nearby Newport, a town we only knew as the place with all the mansions. The agency nibbled, then interviewed, then interviewed again. A couple of days later I pointed out the black-and-white warbler to Shan in that neighborhood pin oak, and hours after that Karen called. She'd taken the job, accelerating life even further.

We drove to Newport and found an apartment, deciding on the way back that we should marry. Karen's last work day would be October 30th, and we invited immediate family to come to an East River park on Halloween. After brief traditional vows at the end of a pier, a cousin of Karen's pronounced us. In from Arizona, my dad was the best man. Karen and I took turns rocking Shannon throughout. The next day we moved, packing what we had in a truck and heading north. If we didn't know what we were driving towards, we did know by now that each of us could take quite a punch, quelling what new-start nerves we might have had.

IF ALASKA HAD LOST A TOUCH of its mystic properties once I actually lived there, Rhode Island provided a
reciprocal effect. Low expectations may have contributed,
but in short order I grew to love the place, a great relief
given that another trapless, fatherless Thanksgiving had
passed, something there wasn't time to dwell upon. If all
new parents are unprepared I was exponentially so, still
perplexed by an increasingly uptight Shannon. Uncertain
of everything from floor time to phonetics drills, I only
knew what mobility did for our daughter, and nearly
every day right through winter walked her over and across
Newport then back and again, then repeat, finding it a far
more intriguing place than I'd imagined. The mansions
were certainly there but were mostly living museums now,
with much of the town covered in diminutive colonial
homes that had housed everyone from whalers to admi-
rals to pirates to religious dissidents to slave traders to

slaves to Revolutionaries. I'd cached myself in Whoville for so long that I'd forgotten what a snarled, spectacularly interesting place America really is and, first through Queens and then through Newport, was happy again to cat-paw such past-present ravelments.

When the weather broke in March, I incorporated at least a couple of beach hours most days, noting the joy that sand brought to Shannon's bare feet. Having just started walking, she did so on her toes, twisting them into soil and sand whenever shoeless. Shorebirds were back, migrating through, followed three months later by vacationers. Undaunted, even stimulated, Shan would run from one end of the shore to the next, slaloming sun-bathers, with life scampering by just as fast. By July Karen was pregnant again, and only six months later therapists confirmed what I'd first suspected on Halloween, our first wedding anniversary.

The last day of a balmy Indian summer, I'd walked Shannon down for a final beach day. Oftentimes the tides lump red kelp all over, smearing it in great tenth-of-a-mile swaths. Most people avoid it but Shan loved it, postholing for an hour or more the way others walk deep snow—up to the knees. I let her explore. She was nineteen months old now, and I could no longer ignore that kids far younger than her were jabbering on the playgrounds while for the past few weeks Shannon had stopped even looking at Karen or me. If some parents are the first to know, others are the last, but by now even I'd caught on. As she trudged through the seaweed, bending for a crab claw here, a gull feather there, I called her name, then again, repeating until she was forty yards off. She never turned. "She'll be a poet," I thought, throwing up a last-ditch alternative, but I finally knew better.

The next week therapists came to the apartment, speech and occupational, and though they officially declared her the next month, their faces said it all the first time they walked through the door. Autism it was, and life pressed on. After twenty-four hours of bafflement and self-pity, wondering why God hated us, Karen and I recoiled, leveraging both our strengths. A warm, fun-loving woman, Karen is additionally a two-legged spreadsheet, excelling at research and administration. Within days she enrolled Shannon in deeper assessments and intensive therapy regimens. For my part, I tossed our daughter out into the world during all her free hours, taking her everywhere from beaches to forests to malls to meadows to crowded streets. Whatever autism is, it can render the afflicted terrified of the world and everything in it, and I aimed to blast that out of Shan from the start, unsure what good it might do but going that route nonetheless. Conceptually, at least, it was the same as raising any kid—you studied all you could, but in the end went by ear, knowing you'd never really know.

By March, just after Shan turned two, Karen delivered our second, named Flannery for the great Georgian stenographer. More mayhem ensued, with time somehow speeding further ahead, but as bizarre, unpredictable, chaotic, and unnerving as autism can be, we absorbed its plaintive vagaries and distorted elations as just another part of our lives, one that for all its wild kinetics continually provides insights inaccessible to any outside the tribe. We called Shan "Eve Before the Fall," and she may be just that: a window into a time when human and animal weren't distinct, prior to custom, language, and guile becoming the hands that made us more art than clay. God may not send such people, but Karen and I needed to believe otherwise, and always will.

May brought a respite, though bittersweet. Sale of the lake cottage where I'd spent so many childhood summers had become imminent, as it became increasingly clear that no one in the family would be able to spend time there. Taking a mid-May weekend, Karen and I took the kids for a final go-through, allowing me what I expected would be a series of silent goodbyes.

Though we drove along the Starrucca, its briar-choked banks weren't proper for a toddler and baby. For that I chose the Equinunk, a similar-sized stream but one tightly penned by mountains, lacking the valley bottomlands—and subsequent farms—of the Starrucca. My dad and I had often trapped there too, along with hunting its grousy ridges, but mostly I remembered it for trout, accruing legions of childhood memories between its banks. The mountains forced the dirt road tight to the creek, and as it receives next to no traffic, Karen and I were able to walk the girls comfortably along. Water had always stilled Shan, and holding her most of the way I could look off the high bank into a vat of pleasing recollection.

Some memories that you don't live, of course, are clearer than many that you do, the dowry of gifted story-telling. With Karen and Flannery wandering a bit behind, I summoned up one such image that I'd pictured hundreds of times before. The Equinunk I could always see, down to the last sycamore, as I'd spent so much time there, but there's an old fisherman's face I always have to sketch in, though the face isn't the gist, just that clutch of wet flies—Dark Hendriksen's—that he handed my pop long before I ever tagged along.

My father opened me up to it in this valley, all of it, starting with fishing. He moved his arms gently with my own, teaching to lay a fly just above each riffle. His patience never frayed, not ruffling if I snagged a willow or even his shirt. Eventually a few fish were caught, and he moved water back and forth across their weary gills.

"Take your time," he said. "They'll revive."

He turned rocks over, fingering the strange creatures beneath, delving each one.

"Mayfly. They're the most common here. Many kinds."

Worlds were under those rocks. Stoneflies, caddis, drag-onfly nymphs, and more. The Equinunk was the first place I held a hellgrammite.

"Take it," my dad said. "Let it walk around your palm. They're fine. Trout love them."

The sound of that stream and the sound of his voice were tough to separate, and still are. My father knew such places from experience. His father gave him the groundwork, but every watershed has its nuances, and he learned this one through his own dedication to place. The Hendricksen's, though, were a gift, a gift with a dowry all its own.

LATE MAY. That's the time. I was ten, maybe eleven, having fly-fished for two or three years, often enough to know that this was the last weekend the smaller creeks would be productive. After this the great insect hatches would fizzle out, and dwindling flows would make fish wary.

We parked by the old, metallic suspension bridge, the same one by which, years later, Karen and I would leave our car. Normally my father walked up a couple of miles, fishing down, while I worked downstream from the bridge, walking up later. This day was no different. We fitted our rods together beneath overcast skies while a few duns fluttered up from the creek, tannish wings suspending gray, bent-back bodies. My dad held out a finger, gulling one to land.

"Clip your flies," he said, reaching into a pocket for a fly box and removing a half dozen.

I put my hand out and he dropped them in my palm.

They didn't look much different than the others I'd seen, just the pattern—size 12 hook, gray fur wound about the shaft, tan feathers with delicate brown barring coming out from the eye.

"Don't change flies. You won't have to. They won't hit anything else today."

He re-did his own set-up alongside me, then said, "Keep a tight line" as he strode away to start his long walk.

Once in the creek I stripped line from my reel and looked about. Insects—identical to the others—floated off the current, like snow falling backward. By mid-May most of the hatchery fish have been caught. Native brook trout, too, have been relegated to the headwaters for decades, pushed out by browns and rainbows that had originally been stocked but now claim residency. The rainbows are transients, coming up from the Delaware every spring to spawn before returning, a little like salmon, minus the ocean and the dying. My dad once explained the history of the non-natives here.

"They've been here for generations now," he said. "Native enough. Like us."

With the duns now clouding off the water, I waded into the creek and casted. The flies hadn't been wet a second before one vanished. I reared back, lurching the rod high, watching a rainbow fling itself airborne, then three more times. They burn up quickly this way, and I stripped this one in close. Cupping a hand beneath its belly, I took in the dense black pearls clustered along the green back from snout to tail, then nudged the side with my thumb, tipping it over. Silver bars the length of the body encased the rainbow-streak between, with tiny scales picking up the dull light to set each platelet twitching—now pink, now rose, now a wavering red. It had a smooth, female face, and I wondered how far upstream she'd go before routing out a nest. Pinching the hook, I slipped it out, then turned the body to face the current, moving her back and forth. A few seconds later she glided from my open palms, flicked her tail, and was gone. I looked to the next riffle, re-casting, watching the flies sail through a firmament of living duns.

Some days it seems like anything but fishing. You hook a trout, let it go, cast, catch one more. As I worked my way down—eddy-pool-riffle, eddy-pool-riffle—there wasn't a stretch that didn't produce, with the bird life now matching that of the fishes' for frenzy—warblers of all kinds, along with a Baltimore oriole and scarlet tanager to enrich the coloration. The wet flies—I didn't know what they were called yet—were well-tied, but the one on the bottom started to fray, the gray-wool body puffing a bit as the fibers unbound themselves. No matter. Fish hit it just the same.

It wasn't quite dark when I finished the two-mile walk back to the bridge, but it was close. My father had a final pool to fish, and I climbed down the bank, waiting for him on a current-worn oak at water's edge. The hatch had crested, but insects still poured off the water, with bats now overlapping the birds.

Upstream, my pop had challenges. Winter floods had jammed several logs in the pool he now fished, an obvious nook for trout but one on which hooks might easily snag. He had lousy vision even then, but for some things he nearly didn't need it. I watched him, but already knew what I'd see. His rod moved skyward, then paused. The leader curled inches from a brace of willow catkins and he brought all forward, landing the lead hook just shy of the outmost log. The rod snapped back and a rainbow shimmied from the current. A small fish, he worked it through two more jumps before bending forward for the release. When it recovered he stood, wading over to join me on the oak.

"The Hendricksen's work ok?" he asked, sitting.

"Is that what they're called?"

"Yeah. Dark Hendricksen's. They hatch about this time every year. We've just missed them the last couple of springs. I knew we'd catch up with them eventually."

A bat whispered overhead, while a trout splashed in the creek, followed quickly by another.

"The first time I hit this hatch it was just like this," he said. "I went at it all day with fish jumping everywhere, hours on end, but didn't catch a thing. I worked from up top down through to where you probably stopped, skunked the whole way."

It was tough to imagine fishing a day like this and not catching anything, but I listened, lightly pinching a dun's wings from my forearm, releasing the bug at arm's length. My dad went on.

"Finally I caught a little brownie. I put him back, then noticed a guy fishing down through where I just had, an older guy. He caught a half-dozen without breaking a sweat, rolling casts into the same square inches of water I'd just pounded without a nibble. I sat on one of those big, bleached boulders down there and watched. He took his time, releasing every fish but one, the last a nice rainbow he slipped in his creel before coming over."

Early summer has a long, friendly twilight, and sitting on that oak my dad and I enjoyed the last wisps of it beneath a burgeoning Milky Way. I was used to my father being the teacher, not the student. This story had legs.

"He might have been sixty, but back then that was over twice my age. I didn't dare ask what he was using, but he wondered how I'd fared and I told him. 'Here,' he said, showing me the fly stuck in his rod cork. 'This is what you want.' I didn't know it then, but it was a Dark Hendricksen, the same we used today. I talked to him for an hour or more. Most guys are tight-lipped, but this one loved the woods and loved sharing what he knew. It turns out that he tied his own flies, making the Hendricksen wings from woodcock he'd shot in this same valley, while getting muskrat fur for the bodies from a friend who trapped. He gave me a few and said they hatched about this time every year. That was it. Every season since I've tried to be here on the right day."

My father told me that story thirty-five years before, but it's often the softer tales, the ones where not much happens, that leave a mark. Looking off the road, holding a current-riveted Shan tight to my body, it seemed like I'd absorbed that imagery only minutes ago, and with my life now a far different thing, I re-assessed.

An older guy caught some fish. Though his generosity has staying power, that's only a fraction of it. It was the feel he had for the woods, not like a man out there but as something that belonged. Even as my father described him I could see the figure moving over creek stones like water, then soft October footfalls in the birch and apple duff, surveying landscape, knowing woodcock. Not much noise, no fuss at all. He may have had nothing to do with this valley, but this valley had everything to do with him, and as I now pictured that figure moving downstream, working at hands with the watershed, it was no longer a stranger I saw, but my dad.

Lowering Shan to the dirt road, I guided her down an easy access to the creek. Karen followed after, Flannery asleep on her chest. At two, Shannon's feet had more surety, and I let her stumble about the stones, then into a soon-to-dry pool left by receding waters.

I never thought I wouldn't hunt, fish, or trap, but with kids the nursery years require abeyance. Not realizing until Shannon was born what my own dad had given up, I worked the chronology over and again before at last understanding. For years he limited himself to a hunt or two each fall, maybe a couple of trout stints per spring, but for the most part lived as if kids are owed the greater share, which of course they are. If I were to ever ask him, he'd also say that they're owed the woods. If there are many things you can't do with a toddler, you can certainly set them free in the ferns a while, encourage tossed stones in a creek, and along the Equinunk Shannon did just that, repeatedly bending for properly-sized projectiles, reveling in the splashes they made.

"Throw," Karen and I said, and she did.

So much of what I'd learned, I'd learned right here, here and places just like it. Connecticut or Pennsylvania, even Vermont into adulthood, were wonderlands, with their creeks and hills becoming rivers and mountains unknown, myth-makers. As happens, though, in time they came to seem ordinary and, spurred by lifelong visions of many elsewheres, I'd done what itchy Americans have always done, went West, hoping to see the light and space of the world. It was certainly there, and what I'd left behind grew ever more pedestrian even as I maintained an emotional reverence for it. Standing by that Equinunk pool, however, all that initial wonder flooded forth, and I realized right then what light and space really are.

Most of us, then, form on land outside the American dreamscape, experiencing vital interaction with features neither mountain nor river, but the simple swales, draws, rivu-lets, and hilltops that comprise the bulk of where nearly all of us live. If not the Tetons or Denali, the Grand Canyon or the Columbia, there is no such thing as ordinary, and the nexus of flesh and spirit oozes from an Equinunk mayfly the same as it does a Kodiak brown bear. I looked down, at Shannon, still pitching stones, then to Karen and Flannery. I didn't need to say goodbye to a thing.

It REALLY ALL is right there, all the time.

Newport has a park, small, topping a hill above the harbor and bustling tourist section. Named for Isaac Touro, prayer leader of the Sephardic Jews who erected one of America's earliest synagogues, it's a quiet place, one Shan enjoyed. She'd jog from tree to tree, fingering bark, pressing the bare balls of her feet into mown grass. Without speech we were free to engage in other ways, oftentimes simply wandering into our own private inquiries.

A stone structure anchors the park, resting on eight pillars, flat rock stacked atop flat rock, over thirty feet high. No one knows what it was. A mill many guess, others a watch tower, but mystery is the only certainty. Some even think the masons were pre-English—Nordics, maybe, or Basque fishermen. Whoever they were, they built something, something that has lasted.

"Don't just punch a clock," my pop had poignantly tendered when Shan was born. "Make something."

That was certainly his approach, and if first Shannon's arrival, then Flannery's, had derailed our traditional endeavors, the exchange was obviously worth it. Besides, on his visits we now had their company, pointing out mallards, brant, canvasbacks, and others off of Rhode Island's shores, along with the fluttering and crawling everythings within its hard and soft woods.

For the rest, we had forty years of memories grouted in place, not unlike the Touro tower. If they wouldn't last four hundred years, they'd last through those remaining to us, providing more wall than we needed to hold us up. Whatever else we'd been doing in the woods all that time, that was probably the most of it.

As for God, my peculiar thirst for verification never slaked, only modulated. For some people, most maybe, such presence radiates the core, like the earth's, driving everything up top. As I'd finally realized along Yakutat's East River, that undoubtedly includes me, though something had changed. Whether it was fatherhood, marriage, Shannon's condition, simple ageing, or everything in combination I didn't know, but I'd come to more peaceable terms with uncertainty.

Whatever God may or may not be, then, the concept itself relieves our timeless bewilderments, all centered on mortality. What happens when we die? Nothing? A sweet hereafter? Hell? For all the suffering it inflicts, the world—specifically the memories and relationships we acquire within it—is far too astonishing for most of us to ever want to leave, and life's continuation by any means has been our greatest tonic, fabricated or not. At some point, though, a simpatico alliance with uncertainty might enhance our enjoyment of all things, for as in parenting, as in marriage, as in living in general, in the end you go by ear, knowing you'll never really know.

The weekend after we'd gone to the Equinunk, Karen and I each took a kid one morning. I took Shan, to later join up with Flannery and Karen at the beach by her aunt and uncle's house. Shannon had always been taken with forests, and I spent a few hours at a favored nature preserve, centered on an old mill pond locked in by a hundred-year old mix of oak and white pine. My pop had visited several weeks before and we'd taken Flannery there, noting the pine warblers staking out courtship zones high in the evergreens, while along a wooded but still leafless path we hovered Flan over something neither my dad nor I had ever seen—a snake, a garter, giving live birth. Unsure of the forms unraveling beneath her, Flan grunted, then again, before looking to each of us for a clarification we could never provide.

Now in late May, with the leaves unfurled and the young-of-the-year well on their way, I geared for Shannon's legs. Ever the water-witch, she by now knew where the pond was, and ran the trail toward it. Beavers had beefed up the century-old mill dam, adding one beneath it, and I took Shannon below all that to where the water ran free. Frogs were here, and catching one I let her hold it. As she always did, she put her tongue to the slime, then cupped the whole for a few minutes and stared. Occasionally I drizzled water along the creature's moistened skin, then finally pried it from her and tucked it beneath a cut, mink-happy bank, picking her up to divert her elsewhere.

Aided by the well-kept trail we circled the pond, listening to burgeoning bird life. Wading at the inlet, Shan attracted a dragonfly. The azure body and green-globular eyes hovered just before her, judging, before she reached a hand out to send it skyward. With the organism dazzling off on the design of four independent wings, Shannon followed its flight, then re-focused on her stream-bound feet. With the day half gone, I hoisted her up and headed us for the beach.

Not quite summer, and overcast besides, the shore was mostly ours. Karen's aunt and uncle hadn't opened the cottage yet but didn't mind if we parked there. When Shan and I came out of the sedge I could see Karen holding Flannery in her lap a hundred yards to our right, but as she always did, Shan broke left and ran, full-striding just outside of the tide lap for a mile or more. Turbulence always roused her, and she adored this beach's open-ocean swells, far wilder than Newport's bay-tucked shores.

Worn at last, Shannon stopped, taking a few seconds to splash in the waves before walking back toward the sedge. In the wrack, though, a large, white mass pulled her like a moth. She'd found a gannet, a snake-necked, goose-sized seabird rarely seen from shore.

Grabbing a wing, her hands eased down the stiff, salt-sanded pin feathers before finding its body. She sat, fingering breast-down, belly-down, back-down, with a few sand fleas hopping before the furrows she made. I put my own fingers to it, testing. Firm flesh, the eyes scarcely glazed within the pale yellow head, it was maybe twenty-four hours gone, and I let her at it.

Such digressions could last, I knew, but it was Sunday and getting up on solstice. We had time. Settling down in the sand next to her, I looked right, westward. Karen must have seen us. Though a distant speck, she walked our way, holding Flan, pointing to things, becoming larger.

Offshore, a glob of gulls harried a trawler, a boat likely dragging up skates for lobster bait, while a few recreational craft worked troll gear just outside the breakers. Stripers, I guessed, but didn't know. Shan lifted the bird's head, fingering an eye, now the bill, then worked down its considerable neck, rolling fine, fur-like plumage between thumbs and forefingers as if embroidering. Somewhere in that motion I noticed the sag. Gannets are fish-eaters, flocking in enormous patrols, plunging whenever larger fish chase mackerel and bunker to the surface. In all likelihood this one broke its neck on such a dive.

Minutes passed, then more, with Shannon seeming to fondle every feather. The rising tide piled successive swells upon the sand not far before us, but even these thunderclaps—normally so seductive—couldn't pull her off the bird, though something far subtler did.

Most shorebirds had moved through, but a few, including these Least Sandpipers, still lagged on their way to the Arctic. Fifty or so had whisped overhead, then wheeled for another pass, this over the surf. Nearly skimming water, they peeled toward the beach and turned, gliding by us. It was tough to get Shan's attention, but the pattern and motion now before us had her fixed. The flock broke in unison several more times, banking in revolutions, flaring first brown-white then white-brown before heading downshore. Whether such murmurations are piloted or acephalous none as yet know, but as we watched the birds disappear, I touched a hand to my child's shoulder and pointed with the other, speaking as much to myself as I did to her.

"Look, Shannon. Just look."

ACKNOWLEDGMENTS

In addition to my father, wife, and immediate family, I owe thanks to Michael Charney, owner and editor of Riddle Brook Publishing, along with Harry Golden and Tom Gilburg, both football coaches by trade, but, through who they are, have meant a great deal more to a great many people. Thanks are also owed to both Franklin and Marshall College and San Francisco State University, along with the happy few editors of magazines, presses, and university journals who still consider unsolicited submissions. My deepest gratitude is for my daughters, Shannon and Flannery, through whom the world has made a great deal more sense, and a final nod goes to Herman Melville, Robert Frost, and Emily Dickinson, the Holy American Trinity, through whom the world grows ever more confusing.